Back to Your Spiritual Future

The 1994 Chapel of the Air 50-Day Spiritual Adventure "Daring to Dream Again"

Never Too Late to Dream, by David Mains. Discover how to break through the barriers of your past and prejudices, your self-centeredness and anxieties, and reclaim the dreams God has planted in your heart. Book includes group discussion questions. Catalog no. 6-3203.

Back to Your Spiritual Future, by Steve Bell. As the author remembers the highs and lows of his own continuing spiritual journey, he also shares biblical principles and insights to help you refocus your priorities and get back to your spiritual future. Includes individual and group work sections. Catalog no. 6-3205.

How to Be a World-Class Christian, by Paul Borthwick. You can be a part of God's global action—from your own neighborhood to the "ends of the earth." Special 50-Day Adventure abridged edition. Catalog no. 6-3204.

Adventure Journals. Dig deeper into the adventure with day-by-day personal growth exercises. Available in the following editions:

Adult	Catalog no. 6-8830
Student	Catalog no. 6-8832
Children, grades 3–6	Catalog no. 6-8831
Critter County Activity Book	Catalog no. 6-8833

ALSO AVAILABLE

Church Starter Kit	Catalog no. 6-8838
Children's Church Leader's Guide	Catalog no. 6-8836
Small Group Starter Kit	Catalog no. 6-8839
Student Leader's Guide	Catalog no. 6-8828

Steve Bell

VICTOR BOOKS

A DIVISION OF SCRIPTURE PRESS PUBLICATIONS INC.
USA CANADA ENGLAND

Copyediting: Jerry Yamamoto; Barbara Williams
Cover Design: Scott Rattray

Library of Congress Cataloging-in-Publication Data

Bell, Steve (Steve B.)
  Back to your spiritual future / by Steve Bell.
    p.   cm.
  ISBN 1-56476-205-X
  I. Title. 1. Spiritual life—Christianity. 2. Bell, Steve (Steve B.)
BV4501.2.B3923   1993
248.4—dc20   93-33065
                                                                    CIP

---

1 2 3 4 5 6 7 8 9 10 Printing/Year 97 96 95 94 93

DEDICATED TO
my spiritually sensitive wife
VALERIE BURTON BELL
whose pure heart,
refreshing honesty,
and sincere commitment to Jesus
continually encourage me
to dream God's dreams.

Contents

Preface 9

1. Courage to Reform 11

2. Out to Change the World 23

3. Instant Results 39

4. The Seduction of Success 55

5. Dissatisfied 73

6. Tearing Away the Mask 89

7. Choosing to Take Risks 107

8. A Strong Finish 127

Preface

For many Christians, spiritual vitality seems like a lost dream. A number of years ago that was true for me. But not anymore.

In this book I want to share with you my journey toward spiritual reformation or personal revival. It's a journey that began in the late '70s when I started to face myself honestly and admit I was spiritually needy. And it's a journey that's still in process. So I don't come to you as the authority or final word on the topic, but as a fellow struggler with an intense desire to become the person God wants me to be.

What I have to say doesn't come from textbooks, but from my own experiences intermixed with biblical principles and insights I'm learning to infuse into my life. I'm not exaggerating when I say writing about these experiences has definitely been the most challenging and intimidating project I've ever undertaken, primarily because it's been an exercise in self-exposure.

Please understand that I trusted Jesus Christ as my personal Savior at the age of ten. It was a genuine conversion, a decision that really took root. My sins—past, present, and future—were forgiven. My salvation was secure. And in the years that followed I developed a close relationship with Jesus that grew and flourished into my late twenties.

As time passed—and I'll be more specific in the chapters to follow—I became sloppy in my personal spiritual disciplines. Though my faith never wavered, frankly, my hard pursuit after God became sidetracked. It was as though I had gone backward spiritually.

No, I didn't step into some Hollywood time machine as Michael J. Fox did in the movies, but I got off track just the same. Of course, after a series of adventures and misadventures, both Michael J. Fox and Christopher Lloyd eventually returned *Back to the Future*. Eventually, I went back on track as well—back to my *spiritual* future.

If you sense that your spiritual life is a bit stymied or has stalemated, or perhaps you'd say it's literally going backward, then it's my prayer that this book will help you assess where you are, so you can refocus and get on with it—back to *your* spiritual future!

Steve Bell
Summer 1993
Wheaton, Illinois

Chapter One

Courage to Reform

KEY BIBLICAL TRUTH:
Personal reformation can begin
once we find the courage to
admit we're spiritually needy.

*I*t takes courage to be honest.

It's difficult to say to a son or daughter, "When you were young, you were the victim of poor parenting. *I* was the one most responsible, and I was wrong." That takes courage.

How many could say to an employer, "I misrepresented the facts. My report was inaccurate. I lied." It takes incredible personal mettle to make such statements.

I've always felt—along with many others around the country—that in the early '70s, Watergate would have been a nonissue if President Nixon had come forward early and explained to the nation, "A gross impropriety has taken place. I am the one most responsible, and I beg your forgiveness. I pledge to you, the American people, that this matter will be dealt with quickly and fully; and I promise, under my leadership, nothing like this will ever occur again."

Had Richard Nixon taken such a posture, chances are he would have completed his second term in the White House.

It always takes courage to admit, "I was wrong." Those words are hard to say.

To be perfectly honest, however, there's a part of me that

identifies with the approach Mr. Nixon took because I know that acknowledging failure openly is intimidating. Beyond that, I have discovered that admitting personal responsibility for wrongdoing *to myself* can be even more difficult.

Confronting Personal Sin

An example in Scripture of this inability to *own* the truth was when the Prophet Nathan confronted King David concerning David's illicit affair with Bathsheba. You probably recall that David arranged for the battleground death of Bathsheba's husband, Uriah the Hittite, to cover his sin.

Though David had the established reputation of being "a man after God's own heart," it's clear that during this time in his life his heart had become hardened. He's a classic example of a believer who refused to find the courage to admit his misdeeds—especially to himself.

Nathan told David the following story, hoping he'd catch on quickly and come clean:

> There were two men in a certain town, one rich and the other poor. The rich man had a very large number of sheep and cattle, but the poor man had nothing except one little ewe lamb he had bought. He raised it, and it grew up with him and his children. It shared his food, drank from his cup and even slept in his arms. It was like a daughter to him.
>
> Now a traveler came to the rich man, but the rich man refrained from taking one of his own sheep or cattle to prepare a meal for the traveler who had come to him. Instead, he took the ewe lamb that belonged to the poor man and prepared it for the one who had come to him (2 Sam. 12:1-4).

It's apparent from the text that David was attentive to the story because he became furious. The Bible says David burned with anger against the rich man, and then he said to Nathan, "As surely as the Lord lives, the man who did this deserves to die! He must pay for that lamb four times over, because he did such a thing and had no pity" (vv. 5-6).

Obviously, David hadn't personalized the prophet's words. It wasn't until Nathan directly confronted David with the statement, "You are the man!" that David acknowledged the heinousness of his wrongdoing. (And we know David had been in this spiritual predicament for nearly a year or more, because the illegitimate son conceived with Bathsheba had already been born by this time.) After God's word through Nathan pierced the hardness of the king's heart, David was forced to face the truth about himself.

For the first time in months, maybe even years, David understood the awfulness of his spiritual condition. Then, almost immediately, he declared, "I have sinned against the Lord" (v. 13).

It wasn't until King David personally acknowledged he was wrong, until he owned up to the seriousness of his offenses in the eyes of God and man, until he finally admitted his condition—that positive change or spiritual reform actually began in his life.

Like Richard Nixon or King David, I too find it difficult to muster the courage to admit when I'm wrong or that I'm spiritually needy. It's unsettling. Plus, part of me resists being vulnerable publicly. That part of me says, "Just keep it between you and the Lord, Bell."

On the other hand, another voice urges me to "Tell the truth, Steve—the whole truth. There are people who will relate and can profit from what you're learning."

And what's the truth? Well, the truth is:

● I'm a man who has regularly known the wonderful reality of Christ's presence in my life. I'm wholeheartedly committed to serving His kingdom in every way I can. Yet at times, I've been more concerned with *people's* perceptions of me than *God's.*

● I am one who has repeatedly seen God answer specific personal prayer requests. Over the years, time and again, He's accomplished on my behalf far and beyond what I could even dream possible. Even so, I've gone through extended periods when I've struggled in my prayer life, as well as maintaining consistency in my private devotional life.

● Although I hold tenaciously to that well-known maxim, "Only one life, 'twill soon be passed; only what's done for Christ will last," almost without recognizing it, my priorities have gotten out of line. So often in the past, I've become preoccupied with *my* agenda, *my* plans, and (as silly as it reads when I put it on paper) I've actually hoped that somehow God would fit into *my* program.

● Another thing I have to admit: I came to a point in my life when I expected spiritual growth just to happen with age — without having to submit any longer to basic spiritual disciplines. Oh, how I've tried in the past to avoid the pain of discipline! I used to resist saying those words, those necessary words of David, "I have sinned against the Lord."

Yet, if a man like King David, who repeatedly experienced the intervention and protection of God in his life, who knew God so intimately that much of his poetry and songs of adoration were preserved in Scripture, if a man of his spiritual stature could wander off-center and develop a hardened heart, if it could happen to a King David, then it can happen to me or anybody. I mean, should we really be all that surprised when spiritual lethargy, stagnation, hard-heartedness (call it what you like) sets in in the life of a Christian? In a perfect world it doesn't happen, but let's be real!

Living in Self-Delusion

Face it. By nature most of us choose the path of least resistance, especially when our personal comfort zones are threatened. Our tendency is to pretend that the spiritual emptiness or vacuum is not there, to blame somebody else when things go wrong, or to act spiritual and hope others buy into our pretense.

However, in the realm of personal spiritual integrity, such approaches just don't work. In this area of life which is at the core of our very being, the center of who we are, there is no other way to stay on target spiritually but to be courageously honest about who we are and where we fall short.

Tragically, some of us who are Christians, right now, are opting to live in self-delusion. Because this is true, I believe there's a huge need for twentieth-century believers (especially here in North America) to experience personal reformation—revival, if you please. But it will never take place—it cannot take place—until believers are willing to acknowledge their spiritual need.

Perhaps you need to come to the understanding, as I did, that *personal reformation can begin once we find the courage to admit we're spiritually needy.* Or saying this same truth another way: Finding the courage to admit we're needy is the gateway back to our spiritual future.

"So, as the Holy Spirit says: 'Today, if you hear His voice [meaning the voice of the Lord], do not harden your hearts' " (Heb. 3:7). Interestingly, this verse is a direct quote from Psalm 95:8, words attributed to none other than (guess who?) King David—this same David whose heart was hardened for a period of time! Since David knew experientially the serious consequences of harboring a hardened heart, I believe he's speaking with incredible intensity here.

"Today, if you hear His voice, *do not harden your hearts.*" The writer of Hebrews picked up on this a little later in the same passage. "See to it, brothers, that none of you has a sinful, unbelieving heart that turns away from the living God . . . that none of you may be hardened by sin's deceitfulness" (vv. 12-13).

Keep a Tender Heart

From this Scripture it's clear that the Lord is asking each of us to keep a tender heart and give attention to what the Spirit of God might be saying to us. We must always give God the freedom to point out where we're spiritually needy.

King David learned to do this through prayer: "Search me, O God, and know my heart. . . . See if there is any offensive way in me" (Ps. 139:23-24).

It's apparent that David began paying attention. He found the courage to own his offenses, to acknowledge his misdeeds. His heart became spiritually tender and remained that way throughout the rest of his lifetime. David went back to his spiritual future. He experienced personal reformation—and we can too!

On October 31, 1517, Martin Luther posted his ninety-five theses to the door of Castle Church in Wittenberg. It contained a list of grievances against the corporate church. His courageous action prompted what came to be known as the Protestant Reformation, which eventually affected all of Christendom.

Of course, God is the Great Reformer, and He's posted a list of grievances at my heart's door. I've mustered the courage to pay attention, and the result has been painfully wonderful! I've gotten back on track—back to my spiritual future—and I recommend it.

Personal reformation began in my life when I found the courage to admit my need. It can happen in your life too!

For Personal Reflection

■ Agree or Disagree with the following statements:

A _____ D _____ ✓ I find it difficult to admit it when I'm wrong.

A _____ D _____ Praying prayers of confession comes easily for me.

A _____ D _____ If everybody in my church felt as close to Christ as I do right now, my church would be a better place.

A _____ D _____ I closely identify with the author's personal description of his spiritual condition on pages 14–15.

A _____ D _____ ✓ Staying within personal comfort zones is very important to me.

A _____ D _____ ✓ At the moment I'd say my heart is spiritually tender.

a tender heart !!!

■ Ask the Lord to help you assess where you are right now.

Areas where I am strong spiritually:	Areas where I am weak spiritually:
_____	_____
_____	_____
_____	_____
_____	_____

■ Review the biblical account of David and Bathsheba in 2 Samuel 11. Especially note David's extravagant efforts to cover up his sin. Also read 2 Samuel 12 where the Prophet Nathan confronts David. Focus on the variety of emotions displayed throughout the chapter. Though you'll see that David repented and was forgiven, be sure not to overlook the consequences of his hardened heart.

■ Invite God's special involvement in your life by praying David's prayer recorded in Psalm 139:23-24:

"Search me, O God, and know my heart; test me and know my anxious thoughts. See if there is any offensive way in me, and lead me in the way everlasting."

For Group Discussion

1. Talk about a time in your life when you sensed Christ's presence especially near. Describe your life circumstances at the time.

2. Recount from Scripture particular incidents in David's life when he experienced God's obvious intervention in his behalf (i.e., God's approval, His special help, His protection, etc.). Begin looking in 1 Samuel 16–20.

3. David was known as a "man after God's own heart." Do you find it more encouraging or discouraging to think that a person of his stature could wander off center spiritually? Explain your answer.

4. Do you agree or disagree with those who say that confession has essentially become a "lost art" in the individual lives of believers in the North American church? Why?

5. What are some contemporary messages we hear from our secular culture that contradict the biblical mandate to "confess our sins"?

6. Most believers take seriously the Ten Commandments (recorded in Ex. 20:3-17) and attempt to live by them. One of the teachers of the Law publicly asked Jesus, "Of all the commandments, which is the most important?" His response was remarkable:

   "The most important one," answered Jesus, "is this: 'Hear, O Israel, the Lord our God, the Lord is one. Love the Lord your God with all your heart and with all your soul and with all your mind and with all your strength.' The second is this: 'Love your neighbor as yourself.'

There is no commandment greater than these" (Mark 12:29-31).

In light of Jesus' standard, how would you say most Christians you know measure up? What changes might need to take place?

7. Think about how *you* "measure up" to Jesus' words in Mark 12:29-31. What is one step you could take to heed Jesus' expectations more closely?

Chapter Two

Out to Change the World

KEY BIBLICAL TRUTH:
*To experience
personal reformation,
believers must reaffirm
the rightness of their original
"first love" intensity.*

H

aight-Ashbury.

The SDS—Students for a Democratic Society.

Hippies.

Yippies.

Beads.

Bare feet.

Kent State University.

Long hair.

The generation gap.

Bring back memories? It was the late '60s. The baby boom generation after World War II was coming of age and beginning to express itself.

Campus demonstrations.

Protests.

Sit-ins.

Walkouts.

Draft dodging.

Flag burning.

It was a new generation, saying collectively, "The world's a mess. Society's unfair. Politicians and big government are the oppressors. The system's got to change!"

This was the predominant cry of the generation in which

I found myself. Defiantly, many in my generation experimented with alcohol, drugs, and promiscuity. "If it feels good, do it!" was the prevalent motto of the day. It was a complicated era.

For the most part, my peers across the country were rejecting the values and goals our parents had spent a lifetime working toward.

The unofficial war ("military action") in Vietnam was escalating. And worse yet, many in this new generation were called upon and expected to risk their lives fighting a battle they couldn't understand and for which they had little or no feeling.

The country was polarized. Causes sprang up everywhere. People chose sides. And most of us in our late teens and early twenties found what was happening very confusing. Fear, frustration, anger, and escapism marked this decade in U.S. history.

The baby boomers were out to revolutionize the world. "The system's the problem. The system's got to change!"

And where was I when all of this was happening? When so many in my generation were getting national attention by flexing their newly found collective muscle? I was right in the heart of Chicago, where so much of the political action was taking place, studying at . . . the Moody Bible Institute! I was definitely out of step with the majority of my baby boomer peers.

A Spiritual World-changer

But I was out to change my world too. And how was I, a small-town, Midwestern countryboy going to change anything? I had no idea, though I was convinced that what the world needed most was *spiritual* revolution.

I was determined to be a world-changer. I held to my convictions with intensity and had concluded: What better way to prepare for spiritual change than to pursue a solid foundation in Bible and Theology!

It was fall 1967. I had been at Moody less than a week when I met Valerie Burton, the girl I would eventually marry. She was blond, bright, *very* attractive, and possessed a zany sense of humor. Probably "spunky" described her best! But at the core of her personality was a spiritual integrity, an eagerness that I found *most* appealing.

We came from similar backgrounds. Raised in modest but strong Christian homes, each of us had experienced childhood conversions and had remained steady in our faith throughout junior high and high school. As I look back, I marvel at the way God preserved and protected us through those teenage years, which typically can be turbulent, experimental, and rebellious.

Our three years of training at Moody Bible Institute brought us together and deepened us spiritually. But also just by living in downtown Chicago, we were exposed up close to the realities of the explosive shifting social concerns and growing political unrest that pervaded the nation.

For a period of time, Chicago was literally under siege by the National Guard during the riots and looting, which took place following the Martin Luther King, Jr. assassination in 1968. Tanks, jeeps, and armed militia roamed the streets. From our dormitory rooftops we watched the fires burning out of control just blocks away on the city's west side.

Months later, during the 1968 Democratic Convention, the student rioting and clashes with police took place in nearby Lincoln Park. That these intensely pitched student protests, involving literally thousands who clamored for national media attention, to think that it was all happening only a few blocks north of Moody's campus was for me, a small-town Ohio boy, a lot to process!

But being close enough to see for myself the anguish, the tragedy, and the horror of such events only deepened my already growing conviction that it wasn't just the *system* that had to change — the change needed most was *inside people's hearts!*

As a student who had chosen a different approach to "world-changing," what I observed while living in Chicago for those years added significance for me to Paul's instructions to Timothy. He too was young and in training at the time when Paul wrote him, "Flee [avoid, stay far from] the evil desires of youth, [instead] pursue righteousness [that's right living in God's eyes] . . . love [as Christ demonstrated it] and peace [which comes only from the Prince of Peace]. Paul went on and told Timothy to do so—that is "pursue righteousness . . . love and peace—with those who call on the Lord out of a pure heart" (2 Tim. 2:22).

Paul's words summarized succinctly my heart's desire, as well as Valerie's. Never did I suspect at that time in my life that I could possibly lose the spiritual intensity I felt so deeply within. I was a determined (but naive) potential world-changer. However, my fervor, my original spiritual excitement, my "first love" relationship with Jesus was, at that time, still very much intact.

Discovering My Personal Mission

In June of 1970, Valerie and I graduated from Moody, and then married two weeks later. Both of us needed two additional years of schooling to complete requirements for our bachelor degrees. I went on to Wheaton College, a Christian liberal arts school in the western suburbs of Chicago, and Valerie entered the American Conservatory of Music in Chicago's Loop. I was still uncertain as to exactly what career I was training for.

We were open to the possibility of foreign missions, as I had been overseas on three different occasions as a teenager serving with short-term student groups. I was also seriously considering medicine. That interest sparked while working for an ambulance service the summer we married.

Just before classes began at Wheaton, through an unexpected recommendation, I landed a part-time job ministering to young people at one of the local churches in the area. It was an excellent opportunity to get close to students (just a few years younger than I) and to influence them toward the Lord. I came to love it!

There we were, newly married, both in school full time, and determined to make ends meet on our own without parental help. I was juggling several jobs simultaneously. I had a daily afternoon school bus route, cut hair one evening a week, worked six nights weekly as a security guard (the midnight to 8 A.M. shift, but I could do all my studying on the job), and yes, I even worked some as a used car salesman! But it was my ministry I liked the best.

My internal juices were pumping fastest when I was working at the church with people. Unlike an older pastor friend who once told me, "I love the ministry; it's *people* I can't stand," I thrived on both! Ministering on behalf of Christ brought focus to the pieces of my life.

The Lord was giving me a burden especially for young people who were raised in Christian homes and products of the church. It seemed that many of these students lacked spiritual fire, that motivation toward the Lord that I sensed so keenly within me. Most of them claimed to have had a conversion experience, but they had lost their original excitement. The intensity of their "first love" encounter with Jesus had noticeably diminished.

In stark contrast to the turmoil I observed in the inner city—where spiritual reality shone brightly against the backdrop of darkness—the comfortable, secure suburbs seemed to be spawning students in the Christian world who had learned to echo all the acceptable God-words without taking them to heart. This glaring gap between spiritual talk and personal experience disturbed me greatly. In fact, it became my mission to do whatever possible to combat this problem.

A Commitment to Spiritual Fervor

This burden or growing sense of calling was cemented in my mind when both Valerie and I were about to complete our undergraduate degrees.

Richard Nixon was winding down his first term in office. He had just returned from his historic journey to China, which opened up a new era in Chinese-U.S. relations. The Watergate burglary had not yet occurred. It was still a month or so before George Wallace was shot while campaigning for President. We were a little more than a year away from the beginning of the energy crisis. It was spring 1972.

One evening, in our small two-room apartment, I remember vividly kneeling with Valerie at the only piece of furniture we owned—a hide-a-bed purchased with wedding money. Together we prayed, "Lord, we'll do anything You ask of us. Location, vocation—none of that matters. Most of all, we don't want to be simply comfortable or mediocre. God, keep us from that. Keep us spiritually hot!"

Little did we know at that time how easily, how unsuspectingly, that internal fire could cool down. Even in us!

Undoubtedly, the possibility of believers losing their spiritual fire was why Paul included in his instructions to the church at Rome, "Never be lacking in zeal, but keep your spiritual fervor" (Rom. 12:11). It's a problem anticipated and dealt with throughout Scripture. And it's a truth I wanted to make certain those church kids understood.

Yet there I was totally unaware that God would someday need to speak those same words to me.

United in a Common Purpose

About this same time I was accepted to Wheaton Graduate School. I had figured out, if I took five classes each quarter (instead of the usual three), I could complete my master's degree in just one year and then get on with life. So that's what I did. Fortunately, my course of study in Christian Ministries and Education dovetailed nicely with my part-time church job ministering to students.

Looking back, it's apparent now that the Lord was uniting our hearts with a common purpose. While I was in grad school, Valerie was teaching at a nearby Christian day school. At the church I was working with teenagers, and we lived in a dormitory full of college women where Valerie served as the head resident director. Our lives were enmeshed in the wide gamut of the student world. And as a couple, we were increasingly aware of their spiritual needs and struggles.

Most of the churchgoing students we worked with could rattle off all sorts of Bible facts. They knew Christian lingo inside and out, could define theological concepts like salvation, sanctification, and even the sovereignty of God. Yet, for the most part, their faith was more in their heads than in their hearts, more academic than personal. As the saying goes, they had been "exposed to just enough Christianity to be inoculated against the real thing."

As I was about to finish graduate school, a specific opportunity was offered to us for ministry overseas. But it seemed that the Lord was confronting us with a wide-open mission field of a different sort right here in North America—prodding students in the Christian world to experience the reality and vitality of a personal faith in Jesus Christ.

The cause Valerie and I felt called to was the process of making disciples. We worked well as a team, both of us were spiritually alert and equally eager to serve Christ in full-time ministry. We had given ourselves wholeheartedly to the Lord, and we were dedicated to those students under our care.

We spent time with them. We encouraged them. We prayed together. In small groups, as well as large, we interacted with the Scriptures. We laughed. We cried. There was rapport, a mutuality. We felt as though we had found a niche in God's kingdom. The Lord was beginning a spiritual revolution in the lives of some of those kids. How thrilling to be a part of it all!

As a couple, we could identify with the psalmist when he said, "My zeal for God and His work burns hot within me" (Ps. 69:9, TLB). And, as is stated later on in the same passage, "The humble shall see their God at work for them. No wonder they will be so glad! All who seek for God shall live in joy" (v. 32, TLB).

The message we felt compelled to share was: *Knowing about* God and *knowing* God are not necessarily one and the same. A faith that's real and impacts the way we live on a daily basis is rooted in an active, personal, intimate relationship with the Lord.

Now what could be more basic? Yet many within the church, and (as I came to discover later) not just students, after initial faith, have settled for knowing facts and truths *about* God in lieu of maintaining a vital and vibrant personal relationship *with* Him.

First-love Intensity

Do you remember what it was like in your life when you first met the Lord? When you were so on fire spiritually? Can you recall that deep love, that excitement, that urgent sense of needing to be with Him? The freshness of Scripture? The privilege of prayer? Your hunger—that desire within you to grow? The boldness when you talked freely about your faith?

Remember how good it was?

Church was a top priority. You actually looked for excuses to be with God's people. Your conscience was clear and sensitive to the Spirit. Time in the Lord's presence was a delight. You were quick to forgive. Not easily offended.

Usually the first to say, "I'm sorry."

Are you relating to any of what I'm describing?

Obviously, the specifics in your life will be unique, but all who have personally encountered the Lord have tasted that original enthusiasm or excitement.

And what about now? At the moment, how would you describe yourself spiritually?

Think of it this way. Compared to your spiritual high watermark, your greatest level of enthusiasm about the things of God—that time in your life when you were willing to do anything for the Lord—if on a scale of one to ten (ten representing when your relationship with Christ was at its peak), how would you rate where you are on that scale right now?

Be honest. Has something changed? Has something been lost along the way?

Of course, the more significant issue here is not simply where *you* would rank yourself, but how would *God* evaluate you?

Your six or seven might be high compared to the crowd you run with. In your setting it might even be good enough to qualify you to serve as a youth leader or a Sunday School teacher. But understand, the only evaluation that carries any clout is what Jesus thinks, based on His criteria.

Addressing believers in the church at Ephesus, Jesus said, "I know your deeds, your hard work. . . . Yet I hold this against you: You have forsaken your first love. [Forsaken your first love—that's *His* criteria!] Remember the height from which you have fallen! [In other words, remember your spiritual high watermark.] Repent and do the things you did at first" (Rev. 2:2, 4-5).

Jesus holds us up before His standard. The intensity of our first love, where we were at our spiritual high watermark, that original excitement isn't to be just a temporary phenomenon—it's the expected norm for all Christians!

Don't believe for a moment the lie of the enemy that

spiritual zeal is only a passing phase, or something for the young or the naturally enthusiastic. Nothing could be further from the truth. Jesus intends for each of us to hold on, to maintain our spiritual intensity.

He tells us to remember (to fix in our mind) when our relationship with Him was at its peak. "Repent . . . " says the Lord. Or said differently: "Do an about-face, turn around, reform your thinking." And then He continues, "Do the things you did [back then]." Return to that original excitement!

In this passage to the Ephesian believers, Jesus was emphasizing the concept of personal reformation. I'm convinced it's the message believers need to hear today more than any other.

Salvation is initial reformation, but God intends reformation, positive spiritual change, to be taking place in our lives continually. And for this to happen, *to experience personal reformation, believers must reaffirm the rightness of their original "first love" intensity.*

Spiritual eagerness, hotness, is to be the norm. The Apostle Paul reiterates this same truth, "Never be lacking in zeal, but keep your spiritual fervor, serving the Lord"—and let me add, with *intensity!* (Rom. 12:11)

And how might we do this? How can we reaffirm the rightness, the normalcy, of our "first love" spiritually? Jesus said, "He who has an ear, let him hear what the Spirit says" (Rev. 2:7). If the Spirit is speaking to you, let me suggest the following prayer of reaffirmation. I invite you to pray it right now.

Lord, I agree that our relationship has been closer in past days than it is now. Either You've changed, or I've changed. And in all honesty, I know the distance is because of me. You have a legitimate grievance against me because I've lost the spiritual intensity I once had. I now understand and reaffirm the rightness of my original excitement. Help me find the courage to make the necessary adjustments to recapture it. I'm needy. Rekindle me. Reignite me. I give You permission, Lord, to be the Great Reformer in my life. Amen.

For Personal Reflection

■ Recall your conversion experience, or that time in your life when you first understood that you were genuinely committed to following Jesus—when you knew you belonged to Christ. List words or phrases below that would most accurately characterize you then:

e.g., spiritually eager _____

open to growth _____

_____ _____

_____ _____

_____ _____

_____ _____

■ In Psalm 69:9 (TLB) David declared, "My zeal for God and His work burns hot within me." What aspect(s) of God's work "burns hot" within you right now? What about in the past?

At present: _____

_____

_____

In the past: _____

_____

■ On a scale of 1 to 10 (10 representing your greatest level of enthusiasm about the things of God), how would you rate where you are at the moment? Mark an "X" on the scale below.

1—2—3—4—5—6—7—8—9—10—

_____

(month/day/year)

■ Note Jesus' feelings expressed to the church in Laodicea in Revelation 3:14-22. Might His words be appropriate for you? As you read the text pay particular attention to verses 15-16 and 19-20.

■ If the Spirit is prompting you—and if it's applicable— rework the prayer at the end of chapter 2 (on pages 33-34) into your own words, then offer your personal version sincerely to the Lord.

For Group Discussion

1. Where were you in the '60s? To what degree were you
   influenced by (and did you participate in) this American
   decade marked by fear, frustration, anger, and escapism?
   Share about what your life was like back then. (If no one
   in your group can remember that far back, invite someone who can share a firsthand report to join with you for
   this session!)

2. Many in the student world of the '60s felt compelled to
   make their voices heard regarding the obvious issues of
   that day. What are some of the obvious issues affecting
   society today? How strongly do you feel about personal
   involvement in these issues? In what way(s) are you making or could you make your voice heard?

3. In this chapter the author talked about discovering his
   personal mission or burden. What cause or concern (it
   might be spiritual or otherwise) do you feel very strongly
   about? Asked differently: When your "internal juices are
   pumping fastest," what specific issue or "arena" are you
   involved in?

4. How realistic an expectation do you think Romans 12:11
   is? Might Paul be "pushing it" here? Explain your answer.

   "Never be lacking in zeal, but keep your spiritual fervor,
   serving the Lord." Or *The Living Bible* translation: "Never be lazy in your work but serve the Lord enthusiastically."

5. What are some of today's "dangers" that loom for students raised in Christian homes and growing up in the

church? How similar or different are they from what the author described in chapter 2? (It might be interesting to invite some high school or college students to join this session to share their personal insights.)

6. Discuss the difference between knowing about God and actually knowing God personally. Think of people you know who fit either category. Describe for the group someone you know who you think fits both categories. What unique traits mark him or her?

7. Contemporary Christian recording artist Steve Camp has written a song titled "Living in Laodicea." If possible, play his song for the group and focus on the words. Then discuss the message of the song. In light of your experience and the people you know, how accurate and/or relevant is it?

Chapter Three

Instant Results

KEY BIBLICAL TRUTH:
*Believers who are spiritually
alive must be careful
to view their productivity
as the result of God's doing.*

Sunny south Florida.
A tropical paradise.
Beautiful beaches.
Fabulous weather.
A year-round outdoor lifestyle.

In one sense, with all the "snowbirds" and people transplants, Florida is really an up-north state down-south. It provides a climate many spend the better part of a lifetime dreaming about, hoping to retire there.

Please excuse me if this is beginning to read like copy for a travel agency commercial. But I have to confess, I love south Florida! And after having lived there for nine years, I guess I still have a little sand in my shoes.

Everyday sunshine. Coconut palms. The salty tang freshness of an ocean breeze. Citrus trees in the backyard. The luscious landscape boasting the ever-present green of neatly kept lawns, accented by a variety of tropical trees, flowering foliage, budding bushes, and exotic plantings too numerous to even categorize.

For Valerie and me, both Midwesterners, it was a whole new world. But we adapted to it very quickly. I think it took us about five minutes to feel at home!

We were excited. In the summer of 1973, a full-time student ministry had opened up to us in a community church in south Florida. Though the church was made up primarily of retirees, they were not of the "rocking chair set" — if you know what I mean.

We were impressed. The people were deeply committed to reaching their community, and especially its growing number of young families and students. As evidence of this commitment, they had recently completed a fully equipped youth center — the newest and nicest building on the church's campus.

Just before our move, a pastor friend razzed me, "Let me get this straight. You're moving to south Florida to work with young people? Come on, Steve . . . there aren't any teenagers there. That area's overrun with a bunch of old folks. It's all retirees!"

Not only was his statement ungracious, it was inaccurate. South Florida was experiencing a population explosion. Palm Beach County, where we lived, was soon to become the second fastest growing area in the entire country. Because of the new and expanding industries taking hold, young families were moving in by the droves.

I'll never forget how I felt my first official day on the job — August 1, 1973. I sat at my desk in my new office confident that I was in the place of God's choosing. Yet my spirit was anxious.

"What should I do first?" I wondered.

"How do I get started at this business of full-time ministry?"

"What if the kids don't like me?"

"What if we don't connect?"

"After all," I thought, "they are of a different stripe than we've been used to. Most of these kids are into surfing and snorkeling, scuba diving and shrimping — stuff I know nothing about, and activities students up north only read about in *National Geographic*."

The standard "uniform" was faded blue jeans, a T-shirt, and flip-flops for guys *and* girls!

I was feeling very out-of-it and insecure. My thoughts wandered. My feelings were mixed.

Then a Scripture verse came to mind: "Being confident of this, that He who began a good work in you will carry it on to completion" (Phil. 1:6). It's a verse I had memorized years earlier, but now its fresh significance gave me needed perspective.

The rest of what happened that first day has escaped me. But the enduring impression of the experience remains. For the first time in my life I knew I was totally dependent upon the Lord.

A Solid Base of Prayer

I had been given some good advice by a friend, Larry Mills, a ten-year veteran of youth ministry with whom I had worked in Wheaton. Before I left he counseled, "Steve, as soon as you arrive at the church in Florida, get to know the older people. I know your job description is ministering to students, but to help you do that effectively, you need a solid base of prayer support. And believe me (he said this with passion!), you'll find it among the elderly!"

His advice made sense. We took it to heart.

Yet, having to cope with my own set of internal anxieties, I wondered whether I could even "cut it" in ministry as a career. Therefore, I was completely unprepared, and never could have imagined, what the Lord was going to accomplish within those initial weeks and months to follow.

One evening, two very unlikely characters walked into our Wednesday night Bible study. I had never seen them before but, of course, I had only been on the job three or four weeks. They walked in late, and their arrival at the youth center startled everyone.

I was taken back by their appearance—rips in their faded

blue jeans and holes in their T-shirts, plus shoulder-length greasy hair. But it wasn't what they were wearing that took everyone else by surprise. It was who they were!

Both were high school juniors, who had established reputations not merely as drug-users, but as drug-pushers on their school campus and in the community. Later I learned that a lot of their dealings used to take place in the church parking lot before and after Wednesday night youth meetings.

What had prompted them to brave their way into our Bible study? They were eager to meet a couple of the girls who were in attendance that night. As the old axiom goes, "Where the girls are is where the boys are!"

Immediately following the study, several adult associates and I beelined our way to meet those two guys. Wonder of wonders: After about an hour conversation, each of them individually prayed, placing their faith in Jesus Christ!

Two of the most unlikely prospects! Everybody had literally written them off as unreachables, untouchables. But that particular evening, when sincerely confronted with the good news of the Gospel (almost in an instant!), their lives were transformed.

This was the beginning of the Lord unleashing His Spirit on the lives of dozens of students in that group.

A Contagious New Faith

Nothing brings more excitement to a gathering of believers than to have brand-new Christians involved in their fellowship. Their very presence adds freshness and life to the realities of faith. Their innocent questions, their natural enthusiasm, their eagerness to learn . . . the excitement is contagious! And very often, the spillover is the most effective stimulator of spiritual growth in others.

Something of significance was taking place. Out of a group of about sixty regulars, every Monday night between thirty and forty of them would show up to go on visitation. They teamed up in groups of twos and threes, going to the homes of classmates, inviting them to come out on a Wednesday night. I had never seen such a group of motivated young people.

And at the front of the pack were those two "unlikelys," the two brand-new believers. They were burdened for the salvation of their friends and classmates, and even their parents.

Over 50 percent of the students involved with us in those early days came from unchurched homes. And almost every week someone made a decision to trust Christ.

In sharp contrast to my previous youth ministry experience, the attitude among these students was to take their faith seriously. Spiritual hotness was the norm. The student leaders appeared determined to live up to the proverb that encourages, "Do not let your heart envy sinners, but always be zealous for fear of [out of reverence for] the Lord" (Prov. 23:17).

I could hardly believe all that was happening. Our numbers had more than doubled in less than a year. Seventy junior high and high school students committed themselves to participate in an intensive fourteen-week discipleship course. More than two absences meant dropping the course—and over 90 percent completed it.

God was at work. I couldn't have been happier. In fact, I was ecstatic! Along with Valerie, my loyal coworker and confidante, the two of us felt like participants in some kind of supernatural script.

Word that something was happening among our young people was spreading in the community. My arrival at the church had coincided with this outbreak of the Spirit, and in some people's minds there was a direct link.

To many, I had become a kind of Christian Pied Piper. People began to pat me on the back. And, of course, what parents aren't grateful when someone comes along and loves their teenager and raises a flag to follow?

From my perspective, however, I knew I had walked into a situation that I did not create. I was still keenly aware of my own insecurities and inadequacies. Yet, mysteriously, in a very short time, our lives appeared to be fruitful.

We believed the Lord was simply honoring our earlier prayer as a newly married couple, "God, keep our lives from being mediocre. Keep us spiritually hot."

Observing the Supernatural

Initially, it seemed apparent to me that God always honored faithfulness with fruitfulness—that productivity was direct evidence of a vital spiritual life. The truth is, I was naive. There was much I had to learn. The Lord was only beginning to school me, but more about that later.

Life was good. I hadn't been at the church all that long before several high schoolers approached me about leading an early morning Bible study and prayer time on the school's campus. Early morning because, due to overcrowding, the local high school was on split shifts. Classes began for juniors and seniors at 7 o'clock.

So, student-initiated, and with the approval of school officials, at least twenty upperclassmen began gathering on campus for prayer and Bible study every Tuesday at 6:15 A.M. This activity continued for several years.

The level of spiritual commitment within the church youth group was remarkable. There was a genuine sense of camaraderie, a bearing of one another's burdens couched in comfortable openness and honesty. A corporate feeling of belonging was evident. Yet outsiders were always welcome. And included in the dynamic was an aura of expectancy, "What's God going to do next?"

For me, the most delightful privilege of full-time ministry was being positioned to observe up-close the supernatural at work. As leader, I always knew what was supposed to happen when we gathered for meetings. I knew the planned agenda. But, oh, the beauty of seeing God's Spirit intervene in unexpected ways!

Without being prompted, it was common for someone to feel led to share freely about a personal struggle; then, someone else would speak up and be vulnerable . . . then another . . . then tears. A person in the group would walk over and put an arm around the one who's broken; then, almost immediately, volunteers offered to pray for the hurting brother or sister.

I saw it happen time and again: spontaneous encouragement, prayers of affirmation, tears, tenderness expressed. Of course, all of these are Spirit-led ingredients of how the body of Christ is *expected* to function. But it can never be programmed by human effort alone.

A Colorado pastor friend, Roger Thompson, captured the reality of this in a *Leadership Journal* article some time ago, where he mentioned one of their weekly church prayers, "Lord, let something happen [in this service] that's not in the bulletin."

And this capacity to perceive God at work in our corporate and individual experience is a vital spiritual issue for each of us.

A Season of Productivity

The Lord had placed Valerie and me in a situation where it was impossible not to notice His supernatural work. So much was being accomplished.

In Paul's second letter to Timothy, he told the young minister to be faithful in preaching the Word *in season* and out of season. Well, we were experiencing a season of productivity.

A bit later in this same text Paul added, "But you, keep your head in all situations" (2 Tim. 4:5). In other words, "Whatever happens, don't lose perspective. Stay focused, and keep the big picture in mind."

Likewise Jesus told His disciples, "Thus the saying 'One sows and another reaps' is true. I sent you to reap what you have not worked for. Others have done the hard work, and you have reaped the benefits of their labor" (John 4:37-38). How I identified with the truth of these words! The results we were seeing were far beyond anything of our doing.

Probably the most unusual happening in those productive early years was in the spring of '75. School officials invited me to give the commencement address at the community's public high school graduation exercises. I was flabbergasted.

Here I was, an ordained minister, asked to speak on a topic of my choice before a guaranteed audience of nearly 3,000 people—including parents, grandparents, relatives, friends, faculty, and graduates. I was thrilled to be asked, and I jumped at the opportunity!

Again, it was student-initiated. Several key leaders in the senior class (from that early morning campus prayer group!) had swayed the "powers that be" to extend the invitation. In fact, five of the top twelve graduates (out of a class of over 500) were leaders in our student ministry—including the valedictorian and the salutatorian.

The speech went very well—or so I thought. A touch of humor, some sound motivational life principles, and then, being true to my deepest convictions, I felt compelled to conclude with a tasteful presentation of the Gospel.

The next morning the local newspaper ran an editorial titled, "The Good News and the Bad News." It began, "The good news is—last evening nearly 600 graduates received their high school diplomas . . . the bad news was—the commencement speaker. . . !"

To make a long story not so long, the editorial became a heated issue. I became the center of controversy in our community. Literally, for the next month, almost every day, there were letters to the editor offering the gamut of opinions regarding the appropriateness or the inappropriateness of a minister presenting his religious convictions at a public school function.

How did all of this impact my ministry? Were the students I worked with embarrassed or ashamed of me? Not at all. "You were great, Steve." "Now you know what it's really like for us Christians over at the school."

When I didn't buckle under the pressure, they took courage. Actually the controversy worked in our favor. Students, parents, schoolteachers, bank tellers, beauty operators . . . the community in general was openly debating spiritual values. You could hardly avoid religious conversations. My gung-ho students were thrilled. Witnessing opportunities abounded. Our group grew.

Despite all the controversy, there was a temptation to glow in the spotlight directed at me. But I managed, in Paul's words, to "keep my head." A verse from 1 Corinthians 3:7 added more perspective: "Neither he who plants nor he who waters is anything, but only God, who makes things grow."

Giving It All to God

I learned a principle at that time in my life: *Believers who are spiritually alive must be careful to view their productivity as the result of God's doing.* In other words, one indicator of spiritual vitality is how quickly do we credit God and discount our efforts when we experience spiritual success?

I don't mean a flippant, "Praise the Lord," whenever something good happens. I'm talking about a deep conviction, a genuine humility that says, "These positive results are beyond my doing. This is God at work."

Now I'll be the first to admit, it's nice to be patted on the back, to receive words of affirmation: "Great job, Steve. You've got to be one of the best youthworkers in all of south Florida!" Such statements massage the ego; but they can also encourage a loss of perspective if taken too seriously.

The truth is, I could have been just as faithful without the positive results. In fact, that may be where you are right now—working hard, but not seeing much fruit. If so, keep watering, keep planting, keep cultivating. And remember: "[It's] only God, who makes things grow."

If, on the other hand, you're in a season of productivity or fruitbearing, then an important question to ask is: Who's getting the credit?

Watch out for statements like:

"You're the best chairperson this committee has ever had. Won't you consider an extra term? Without you, nothing of substance will ever happen."

"Your solos are absolutely outstanding! You should be featured every Sunday. Compared to you, everybody else is just second rate."

"Yours are the most interesting and stimulating Bible classes I've ever attended at this church. What you have to share is so deep and meaty. I think the *pastor* would benefit immensely if he sat under *your* teaching for a while!"

The fact is, it's difficult to maintain perspective while riding the wave of success. That's why believers, who are spiritually alive, must be careful to view their productivity as the result of God's doing.

Corrie ten Boom, a well-known author and popular speaker, was a beautiful example of one who practiced this principle consistently. It was her custom when speaking to large crowds, if she received applause or affirmation, to lift her hands toward the Lord and say something like, "These are bouquets of praise I pass on to You, Jesus."

She had it right. She always kept her head. Even in the spotlight of success, she maintained proper spiritual focus.

If you're a make-it-happen person in your church, or if your personal ministry is being well-received, your efforts are seemingly paying off for the kingdom, then make certain the credit is going where it belongs. Whenever affirmation comes—and it will, when good things are happening—

if not publicly, at least inwardly say, "Thank You, Jesus. I give it all to You." Such a discipline, when practiced sincerely, is evidence of genuine spiritual vitality.

For Personal Reflection

■ Think back on a time in your life when you felt totally dependent on the Lord. What were your circumstances then? What, if anything, is different between then and now?

■ Note below a Bible verse or passage that has especially ministered to you during an insecure period in your life. Then add to that a helpful piece of advice you've received along the way which has made a lasting impression on you spiritually.

Scripture: _____

_____

Advice: _____

_____

■ Do you personally know any "unlikelys" who have placed faith in Jesus Christ? If so, reflect for a moment about what their lives were like before meeting the Lord. Imagine what their lives would be like now had they never met Christ! Of course, God is still in the life-changing business. Jot down the names of three or four present-day "unlikelys" and commit yourself to begin praying regularly for their salvation.

1. _____ 3. _____

2. _____ 4. _____

■ What is it about the group of believers with whom you fellowship that you find most appealing? To make the dynamics even more attractive, what improvements would you like to see? What unique qualities/interests/additives would you say *you* could bring to your situation to enhance it?

_____

_____

_____

■ Assess as best you can the particular "season" you're experiencing at present. Is this a time of spiritual productivity, fruitbearing? Or are you planting, watering, cultivating . . . or have you been on an extended vacation? Be as specific as possible. If it helps, write out your thoughts below.

_____

_____

_____

■ In all situations believers are urged to "keep their heads" (see 2 Tim. 4:5). When it comes to experiencing some form of success, how good are you at crediting God above your own efforts? Circle below the grade you think He would give you in this area:

A+ A A- B+ B B- C+ C C- D+ D D- F

For Group Discussion

1. Share about a time in your life when God used a specific Scripture or comment from a fellow believer to speak directly to your point of need. What was so significant about that particular incident?

2. What are some benefits of having new Christians participate in the life of the church? Is there a downside to their involvement with well-established believers? Explain your answers.

3. Give a synopsis of the conversion of an "unlikely" you've heard about. (All the better if you know the individual personally!) Be sure to include the impact the person's life and decision has made on others.

4. If time allows, review as a group the dramatic conversion account (in Acts 9) of Saul of Tarsus. What qualified him as an unlikely candidate to become a devoted follower of Jesus?

5. Talk about a time in the life of your church, or in your small group, or even on a personal basis, when you were keenly aware of God's supernatural involvement. What was taking place? How did it make you feel? What was best or exciting about it?

6. Share what you appreciate most about your present church situation. Conclude by suggesting one possible improvement where you hope your efforts will make a positive difference.

7. First Corinthians 3:7 reminds us, "So neither he who plants nor he who waters is anything, but only God, who

makes things grow." In light of this text, brainstorm as a group some practical ways individuals can respond when God acts in our behalf—collectively and/or individually. In other words, to ensure that God receives the credit for the good that's come about we could: (Discuss possible ideas.)

8. The eighteenth-century songwriter and revivalist Charles Wesley (1707–1788) wrote one of his best-loved hymns of the church—"And Can It Be?"—within the first year of his conversion experience. It's impossible to sing this hymn without noticing its exuberant tone and almost operatic style. (Actually, it's a difficult tune to sing, but it's so well-known that nobody seems to mind!) Wesley truly captured in this hymn the substance and emotion of his genuine spiritual conversion. Conclude your session by reading through (and comprehending) the powerful words of the text—the theology is wonderful; then, sing together all the verses with gusto! You'll love it!

Chapter Four

The Seduction of Success

KEY BIBLICAL TRUTH:
Spiritual vitality can only
be maintained if you guard
against the distractions
of success.

*I*n all the years I spent in church ministry, I don't think I ever associated what I did or how I spent my time with my income. Ministry to me wasn't so much a job as a way of life. And living in a rented apartment with no dependents meant no distractions.

From the very beginning, Valerie and I were well-received at the church in south Florida. Oh, a few people thought my hair was too long. Others, I suppose, wondered about the maturity level of a minister who drove a Triumph Spitfire convertible—a little two-seater that looked more like an oversized rollerskate than a car.

But within a very short time, the Lord began to work among our students, and exciting things were taking place. We saw many conversions and dramatic growth—not simply in numbers, but in the spiritual depth of the teenagers as well. Initially though, it was the numerical growth that was most noticeable.

The students decided, on their own, to sit together as a group during Sunday services. They chose to sit, not in the back of the balcony, but right down in front—the first nine or ten rows. Even though the auditorium seated 2,000, it was impossible not to notice the growing number of young people at the front of the sanctuary each week.

Spiritual Growth through Hard Work

The key factor prompting *spiritual* growth was our development of an intense study course called "Dare to Be a Disciple" (or DBD). I came out of graduate school convinced that adults make church far too easy for teenagers.

Let me explain. For a student to excel academically in school, it requires sacrifice and concentrated effort: advanced classes, additional reading, demanding research, extra time. Or in the area of sports, the beginning point is always *total* commitment *plus* getting into top physical shape, then honing skills day after day, and practice, practice, practice. The attitude "I'll show up whenever I *feel* like it" just doesn't cut it!

So whether it's academics or athletics, to do well—to excel—requires loads of commitment, extra time, and lots of hard work. Students understand this. In fact, they expect it!

Why then, should our approach to helping young people mature spiritually be significantly different? Many youth programs cater to the whims of teens, just to keep them off the streets, which is little more than glorified baby-sitting. It's my conviction that teenagers are more apt to respond positively to spiritual realities when *seriously* challenged. Involvement in the "appease them" approach has never appealed to me!

The "Dare to Be a Disciple" program proved to be successful. Every year we offered it for fourteen weeks during late winter and early spring.

"Only sign up if you're committed to spiritual growth," I would warn. "Not everybody's going to make it. It will be tough. It involves reading several books, memorizing Scripture, special projects, pop quizzes, targeting nonbelievers for friendship evangelism. More than two absences, and you're out! Sessions will go for two hours every Friday night or Saturday morning."

Response to the concept was incredibly enthusiastic! Over the years, I developed five different graduated courses so students could advance and continue to participate. And out of the DBDers came the core of our student leadership.

In the summers those who had successfully completed the courses were eligible to go on a two- or three-week overseas missionary trip. Not only did they have to earn the right to qualify, but also they had to raise their own funds if they wanted to participate.

Months in advance, the discipleship groups would sponsor various money-making projects: churchwide spaghetti dinners; household rummage sales (church members donated all the items, and a nearby bowling alley donated their parking lot); all-community chicken barbeque feasts with literally thousands attending! They'd even hire themselves out to congregation members to be "slaves for a day." All of this to help earn their way to be short-term missionaries.

This total group effort produced multiple benefits in their personal walk with the Lord and in their relationships with each other—not to mention the value of exposure to ministry opportunities in other cultures.

And of course, south Florida served as an ideal jumping-off spot for our missionary endeavors to different islands in the Bahamas, Haiti, Trinidad, Grenada, Guatemala, Spain, and Peru.

The structure of the demanding discipleship program was balanced by the informality of Sunday nights when we would interact together in homes. The weekly format was simple: group singing, sharing personal updates and special requests, an extensive prayer time, and then the evening would always end with food—lots of it!

Every Monday night featured visitation outreach, Tuesday nights I led the college and career-age Bible study, the junior high and high school students met separately for our weekly Bible studies on Wednesday evenings. Then what happened on Thursdays, Fridays, and Saturdays varied depending on the season. For example, ten weeks out of the year we sponsored a Thursday night community basketball league for teenagers.

Throughout the year, there were always three or four special weekend retreats, as well as beach days, "eatski" outings (what we called water skiing for a day at a lake with an abundance of food!), rollerskating, miniature golfing, go-carting, bike hikes, clam fries, canoeing in the Florida Keys, surfing, snorkeling, tubing the spring-fed rivers of central Florida, cookouts, Memorial Day Youth Festivals (inviting area youth groups to join with us), oceanside Easter sunrise services, maintaining the tradition we started in our community of winning the "Best in Parade" float every Thanksgiving morning, Christmas caroling on the intracoastal waterway, a formal "very classy" spring banquet, "Fifth Quarter" reachout events following a big game at a local high school, attending football games (back when the University of Miami Hurricanes were still "wannabees" and the Miami Dolphins were the powerhouse of the NFL), our own summer camping programs, the "Young Americans" youth choir and "Young Believers" singing ensemble summer tours, our "Live 'til Midnight" concert series—beginning at 10 P.M. (four to six Friday nights a year and featuring artists like Sandi Patti, Steve Camp, David Meece, B.J. Thomas, and the Imperials), our annual Turkey and Super Bowls—flag-tag football games, which pitted the singles against the marrieds on Thanksgiving and New Year's Day respectively, and an annual fall Christian College Tour for juniors and seniors covering 5,000 miles and fourteen schools—all in twelve days!

In those early years, Valerie and I ate, breathed, slept (or didn't sleep!) youth ministry. Wherever we went, it seemed there was always a group following behind.

Now I have to confess, the residual teenager in me thoroughly enjoyed the nonstop pace. I also delighted in maintaining my position as the unbeatable "king of the mountain"—whether it was in Ping-Pong, one-on-one basketball, or tennis.

In the fall of '75, our first son, Brendan, was born. Suddenly, our lives weren't as simple as before.

New Parents with a House Full of Teens

By this time, we had moved from the rented apartment into a house. With the arrival of Brendan, having become a threesome, we altered our lifestyle somewhat. No longer, at a moment's notice, were we able to drop everything and give total attention to whatever happened to pop up. However, we always remained accessible—especially when genuine needs arose. But, once the baby came, we cut back on some of those late-night spontaneous pizza parties.

All along, our home remained a turnstile for people. It was an unusual week if we weren't up past midnight at least two or three times with a house full of teenagers or college students. From the beginning, Brendan had to learn to sleep with roaring laughter, loud music, or just the typical noise and chatter of a group of people enjoying one another in the next room.

We took him with us almost everywhere. Actually, it was pretty easy because there was always an abundance of built-in baby-sitters. In fact, in the summer of 1976 when Brendan was only nine months old, we took him with us as part of a group of twenty-six to spend two weeks in Guatemala doing ministry and clean-up following the devastating earthquake there.

I can't fully explain it, but somehow, the Lord had granted us the special capacity to enjoy teenagers. Beyond that, we genuinely loved them. When they hurt, we hurt. This was true even with the rebellious or fringy ones, who were around exclusively for the fun activities. The Lord enabled us to look underneath the surface to their incredible potential. Each one, completely unique, with the capacity to know God, to serve Him, and to benefit His kingdom—for a lifetime!

With the passing of time came experience. In my heart I knew I was good at what I did. The Lord had skilled me in interpersonal relationships. I read group situations well. I was quick on my feet verbally. I was able to rally and motivate, not just kids, but also parents. Administration and organization came easily. As much as possible I preferred to delegate the detail work and involve others.

I'd put together a large volunteer staff including parents, a few grandparents, college students, and several seminary summer interns. In spite of their diverse backgrounds, a real sense of "team" developed, allowing me to maintain this (what I now realize to be) hyperactive program! But juggling lots of responsibilities was a challenge I thrived on. My life was a flurry of activity and relationships. It was pressure. It was lots of work. But most of all, it was *fun!*

It's fulfilling and exciting to be in charge, to be the leader, when things are going well. And though initially I was quick to credit the Lord, it was extremely difficult to maintain a realistic perspective when affirmation, appreciation, and adulation continued month after month from parents and peers.

With Success Comes Danger

I was considered a make-it-happen person in ministry. It was said of me, like young David, "In everything he did he had great success, because the Lord was with him" (1 Sam. 18:14).

With success, however, comes danger. There's a positive, and also a negative spillover.

After about five years, I was feeling more and more confident in my field. Outside speaking engagements from around the country were coming my way. The people in our church were very supportive and affirming. There were always plenty of dinner invitations.

Every winter requests from grandparents to meet their teenage grandchildren who were down visiting for a couple of weeks on break overwhelmed me. "If they could just get a taste from you, Steve, as to how exciting and fun Christianity can really be!"

Strokes . . . strokes . . . strokes.

On the other hand, I was becoming spiritually distracted—feeling stronger in my skills and natural strengths, and less dependent on the Lord.

When the wheels of success are in motion, there's a subtle assumption that, if the systems are in place, success will sustain itself. But as the former governor of Michigan, George Romney, once said, "Nothing is more vulnerable than entrenched success." I'm sure he didn't have spiritual success in mind when he made that statement, but it still applies.

When I thought I was strong and felt increasingly competent, in reality I was becoming weak and vulnerable. And I was totally unaware of it.

It's true. You can ride on the waves of success for a while. But as one man put it, "The quickest and shortest way to crush whatever laurels you have won is for you to rest on them."

The fact of the matter is that success is not always a friend. In most people's eyes I was a successful youth minister. I was good enough. To some I was the best. But without realizing it, I was losing my growth edge.

All these years later, it's now clear to me that God never calls His people to be *successful*. He calls them to be *faithful*.

Looking back, there's no question, I had been faithful in those early years. I had even been careful to credit God for our initial victories. But I also came to enjoy all the attention, accolades, and accompanying perks. And living in a very affluent part of the country, south Florida's Gold Coast, some of the perks were out of the ordinary!

• "Steve, would you and Valerie be able to join us for dinner on Thursday night in Key Largo? . . . Great! . . . Meet us at the airport at about 6. We'll fly down in our plane. The Club's limousine will pick us up and take us to the restaurant, and we should be back at about 10. Our treat."

• "Listen, Steve, just feel free to come over to the Hotel and Club whenever you can fit it in. We have several professional golf courses. You know, Arnie Palmer used to be the Club's pro! Twenty clay tennis courts. We hosted the Virginia Slims tournament last year. And be sure to bring along your friends, anybody you want! I'm happy to do this for you. Consider yourself my standing guest."

• "Hey, can you two get away for a couple of days in the middle of the week? I know weekends won't work for you, so how about next Thursday and Friday? We'll sleep on our yacht, prepare fresh lobster and steaks on the upper deck's grill. It'll be loads of fun. I'll even bring along my smaller 35-foot fishing boat. Two days of deep-sea fishing off the coast of Bimini will do you two good."

Of course, there's nothing intrinsically wrong with perks. All of us need some now and then just to break up the routine. But, they *can* distract one's spiritual focus.

Basic to our human nature is the tendency to build toward comfort. It's something each of us probably gravitates to. And it's not that comfort's necessarily bad. But when pursuing it becomes a preoccupation, a priority—to the neglect of spiritual concerns—it's a serious problem.

Valerie and I were far from wealthy, and we weren't overpaid. But our church people were very generous to us. It was increasingly difficult not to talk about the extravagances of the good life we were tasting. And at the same time, it was becoming harder to center our attention on ministry and the Lord.

Those who are considered most successful are usually the ones with the greatest opportunities to build toward comfort. And this is just as true for those successful in ministry. The praise, the growing influence, the power, the spin-off possibilities—any of these can displace one's original spiritual zeal. Ironically, it's that zeal which is typically the basis for success in the first place!

Remember David, "a man after God's own heart"? As a young warrior in Saul's army, whatever he was sent to do he did so successfully that he kept getting promoted. The Bible records, "This pleased all the people, and Saul's officers as well" (1 Sam. 18:5). Later, when David became king, the love and adulation he received only intensified. Under his rule the country was flourishing economically, militarily, and spiritually.

David was at the pinnacle of his career, when one spring, "at the time when kings go off to war" (2 Sam. 11:1), David chose an option available only to a successful king. Instead of leaving with his troops, he decided to stay at home in Jerusalem and enjoy the perks and comforts of palatial life.

What happened? He got sidetracked and lost his spiritual focus. It was during this time, when he was riding the crest of success, that he became involved in his illicit affair with Bathsheba—and you know the rest of that story! In reality, David's success was a contributing factor to his downfall.

How could this have happened? Well, he knew he was loved. He certainly heard what people were saying. He probably read all of his press releases and evidently he had begun to believe them.

The Bible verifies again and again that spiritual downfall often has its roots in success—from the lives of Gideon, Solomon, Hezekiah, and many others. The point is: Beware of success. It's not always a friend.

Fix in your mind (and, if necessary, mark it down in red

letter ink and highlight it in yellow): God never calls us to be successful—but to be faithful.

There's a life principle in all of this. *Spiritual vitality can only be maintained if you guard against the distractions of success.*

Understand that spiritual "fast-starters" must also sort through the fluff of all the glory along the way. I found that my initial success in ministry blinded me to my need for continual growth, to deepen spiritually. When other ministers my age were developing basic disciplines to cope in more difficult situations, I was operating under the impression that I was already good enough. Success seduced me.

Of course, I'm talking about experiencing success as a youth minister, which you may not relate to at all. Maybe your success is more in line with King David's. Possibly:

● Promotions on the job are helping you climb the corporate ladder. Now you're the one whose professional acumen and advice are being sought after.

● There was a period when you daily prayed, "Lord, if You'll just help me make a few more sales." And not only did He do that, but you now have your own business, and it's going gangbusters!

● From the time your children were babies, you've prayed Hannah-like that they'd grow up in the admonition and nurture of the Lord. That's happened!

● Way back when, you made an investment—a major financial risk at the time—which has turned into something beyond anything you could have imagined. In fact, it's caused you to flourish economically!

● Over the years you've risen to a position of power and prominence in government, or in the military, or even within your own church.

Whatever your success—past or present—watch out! Success breeds an attitude of "I'm pretty good. I know what I'm doing. I'm competent." Regardless of your sincerity or depth of spiritual commitment, the very nature of success and all its spin-offs encourages self-focus and less dependence on the Lord.

Never Stop Growing

So how is it with you? Are you still basking in the glory days of years ago? Are you still talking about the good ol' spiritual heydays of the past?

Or maybe you're enjoying a ride on a wave of success right now. If so, be on your guard. In actuality, you may be very needy and spiritually *un*successful.

Life's priority for every believer is to follow hard after God. For your own sake, for the sake of the kingdom, *you dare not stop growing.*

The writer of Proverbs 4 stated it this way, "Above all else, guard your heart. . . . Let your eyes look straight ahead. . . . Do not swerve to the right or the left" (vv. 23, 25, 27). In other words, avoid all distractions!

Understand, God is always grieved and (I think) disgusted by anything that distracts us from pursuing Him. Whether it's the pursuit of comfort, which is pure self-centeredness; or an attitude of self-sufficient smugness, which smacks of "I'm good enough as is, I don't need You, God"; or craving people's praise over and above God's approval, our spiritual focus is becoming blurred.

Again in Proverbs we're told, "Blessed [fulfilled] is the man who always fears [reveres, or pursues hard after] the Lord, but [here's a warning!] he who hardens his heart [or he who loses his spiritual focus in the pursuit of perks, praise, comfort, success, whatever] falls into trouble" (28:14).

The biggest struggle I had at this point in my life was *admitting to myself* that I was losing my spiritual focus. I had always been Mr. Committed, Mr. On-Fire. And though I didn't yet realize it, my growth edge was dulling. Success was getting me sidetracked.

How ironic that at the very time I was rightly stressing the importance of basic spiritual disciplines in the lives of our students, I was myself getting a little sloppy maintaining those same disciplines in my own life. As a result, my "first love" spiritual intensity was beginning to wane.

It's significant to note that following his affair with Bath-sheba, it wasn't until *after* David admitted to himself he was spiritually needy that he was able to get back on track. Personal renewal, reformation—or getting back to our spiritual future—will never begin in any of us until we find the courage to admit we're spiritually needy.

What is it right now that may be hindering your pursuit of God? Are there any spin-offs of success distracting you? If so, do you have the courage to admit it? These are questions you alone can answer for yourself.

"Above all else, guard your heart. . . . He who hardens his heart falls into trouble." It's a warning all believers should not ignore.

For Personal Reflection

■ Complete the following sentences:

1. To date, I am probably most competent at _____

    _____.

    [area(s) of expertise]

2. I receive the greatest amount of affirmation from oth-

    ers when I _____

    Same?

    _____

    _____.

3. When I'm having the most fun I'm typically _____

    _____.

    [activity involved in]

4. Some abilities or life skills that come easily or

    naturally for me are _____

    _____

    _____.

5. An aspect of life that I really have to work hard at is

    _____.

6. I sense that God is pleased with me when I _____

_____

_____.

■ In what areas of your life are you most concerned about achieving success? Note your answers below:

_____ _____

_____ _____

_____ _____

■ How would you define your life's dream, your ambitions?

_____

_____

■ In what specific ways are you "building toward comfort" in your life? Understand that your efforts in this regard may be perfectly legitimate. However, consider the question: Might any of these efforts conflict with God's dreams for you? Why or why not?

■ Can you recall a time when experiencing success in one aspect of your life contributed to your downfall in another area? If so, as you look back now with some perspective, why do you think this happened?

■ What issues are you currently facing that could potentially distract you spiritually? Focus first on the obvious ones; then think through more subtle possibilities:

Obvious   More Subtle

_____   _____

_____   _____

_____   _____

■ Is there anything in your life at the moment that is hindering your pursuit of God? If so, do you have the courage right now to articulate it out loud—first to yourself, then to God? (Read 1 John 1:5-10.)

For Group Discussion

1. Share areas in your life where you've tasted some success. (For example: friendships, academics, athletics, raising children, career, finances, natural skills or talents, etc.) Don't be shy. What kind of perks did you experience in the process?

2. Do you agree or disagree with the statement, "The quickest and shortest way to crush whatever laurels you have won is to rest on them"? Why? Discuss the dangers of success you've personally experienced and/or observed in the lives of others.

3. Collectively generate a list of ways people "build toward comfort" today. At what point do these pursuits cross over the line of going too far?

4. King David had it all—God's favor, success, power, popularity, wealth, palatial perks, and on and on. Play the role of psychologist. Surmise what David must have been thinking that motivated him to stay behind in Jerusalem instead of traveling with his troops "in the spring, at the time when kings go off to war." (Review 2 Sam. 11:1ff.)

5. Three Old Testament personalities are mentioned in chapter 4—Gideon, Solomon, and Hezekiah—as examples of how "spiritual downfall often has its roots in success." What successes had each of these men achieved, and in what way(s) did each fall? Investigate Judges 6–8; 1 Kings 1–11; and 2 Kings 18–20. (You may want to select individuals to research this information in advance so they're prepared to share their findings with the whole group.)

6. In what ways have you tasted success spiritually? Do you ever receive strokes or perks because of your ministry involvement? How do you feel when your efforts on behalf of the kingdom go unnoticed?

7. Share one of your dreams or ambitions that you believe God has placed in your heart. (Be sure to mention if it's the first time you've ever stated this publicly.) What obstacles are you facing currently that are hindering its fulfillment? What might be the next step you need to take toward seeing this dream come about?

8. It's important to spiritual vitality to pursue our God-given dreams and ambitions. However, some dreams and ambitions are of another sort. Discuss what C.S. Lewis wrote about "Ambition" in *God in the Dock* (1944), "Answers to Questions on Christianity," ans. 9, pp. 55–56:

Ambition! We must be careful what we mean by it. If it means the desire to get ahead of other people—which is what I think it does mean—then it is bad. If it means simply wanting to do a thing well, then it is good. It isn't wrong for an actor to want to act his part as well as it can possibly be acted, but the wish to have his name in bigger type than the other actors is a bad one.

Chapter Five

Dissatisfied

KEY BIBLICAL TRUTH:
*Christians experiencing
spiritual dullness must learn
not to blame outward
circumstances, but to assume
personal responsibility for it.*

During my early years in ministry, I always liked it when someone from outside the church remarked, "You mean, you're a minister? You're kidding! You don't *seem* like a minister." I can't remember ever asking for any explanations, but I just assumed such statements were intended as compliments.

I was young, approachable, fun-loving, and typically upbeat and cheerful. I'm not sure it was right, but down deep, I really enjoyed it when people reacted with surprise when they found out I was a "man of the cloth." To me, not fitting the stereotype of the clergy was gratifying.

In time, however, it became an issue of pride with which the Lord would have to deal.

I had been working with the young people at the church for over five, going on six, years, which had far out-distanced the eighteen-month national average for a full-time youth worker staying in one place. At this point in my experience, some of the junior high students from those initial years at the church were now off to college and university, and many of the first high schoolers we worked with were into graduate schools and seminaries.

A comment we frequently heard, especially from the students who had been with us through most of their high school experience, was, "College life is *dull* compared to all the exciting stuff we did together as a church youth group!"

The Seeds of Dissatisfaction

Serving as a youth pastor is often perceived by people in the church as a training ground for someday becoming a "real pastor." Many people view working with teenagers as merely a stepping-stone to bigger and better and "more legitimate" arenas of ministry. I have to confess, I always resented such thinking.

You might recall, my original motivation to work with students was to be a world-changer. And what better way, I thought, to affect society for good than to make a permanent spiritual impact on the lives of young people. Many adults are on the downside of life with patterns and mindsets essentially set in concrete. Teens, on the other hand, are still in their formative years with a whole lifetime of experience and influence ahead of them!

As the years passed, however, other people's comments began to affect me. As my "successes with kids" mounted, I became anxious to add some dignity and respect to my chosen field of ministry.

More and more I would hear comments like, "Steve Bell is *great* with kids." Initially, I saw it as affirmation. But after a while (though no one ever said it), I began to read into such statements, "But he doesn't have much to say to adults."

Later this would become a significant personal issue with me. But as much as possible I tried to ignore the inner dissatisfaction I was beginning to feel, but couldn't quite label.

Putting this into writing appears cocky to me now, but after five years at the church—as far as youth ministry was concerned—I felt as though I had *done it all!*

I had started out with guarded confidence that we were
in the place of God's choosing, though personally, I was
scared almost spitless wondering whether or not I could do
the job. That's where I began. Just over five years later, I
was feeling competent and beginning to wonder, "What
should my next challenge be? I'm not sure working with
kids will hold my interest much longer."

Twenty years have passed since I first started working full
time at that south Florida church. Now I can see more clearly that though I verbally gave God the credit for ministry
accomplished, within me there was a growing personal
pride and a longing for recognition—not just in the field of
youth ministry, but beyond that. "Oh, that Steve Bell is
great with kids" became a phrase I hated to hear, because
of what was left unsaid!

What's Wrong Here?

In the process of beginning to sort through some of my
unfolding inner turmoil, the pace and activity of our lives
continued to accelerate. Our social calendar (apart from
regular ministry obligations) was always jammed full.

One summer in particular, literally every Friday night and
Saturday were filled with wedding festivities: rehearsals, re-
hearsal dinners, ceremonies, receptions, and all the accompanying hoopla. A standing joke around the church was
"Steve Bell officiates the weddings; the other ministers do
the funerals."

I'm hesitant to even mention this next part. At one point,
I was actually dubbed the "minister of fun." When I first
heard it, it didn't bother me in the least—because basically
it was true. I was fun to be with. People sought me out. The
areas of ministry in which I was involved were exciting.
Things were happening! In fact, some families were joining
the church primarily because of the youth ministry.

Whenever I slowed my pace long enough to think about

"What next? Where do I go from here?" within my soul there was a restlessness. Even though some of my college friends who visited us from ministry situations in other parts of the country would exclaim, "Bell, how did you ever land this place right out of graduate school? You've got it made here!" I was growing more and more dissatisfied. But I wasn't quite sure why.

No matter how hard I tried to put it out of my mind, I could not escape the gnawing anxiety that something wasn't right. "What is it that's wrong here?" I would ask myself. "Maybe I'm growing restless because I'm not as challenged as I once was, and no one's holding me accountable for what's happening (or not happening) in my life. After all, who's *my* mentor? Who is it that's seriously monitoring me and my personal development?

"Or, maybe it's those labels people are slapping on me: 'minister of fun'—that's not a compliment; 'he's great with kids'—as if I have nothing to say to grown-ups. Do you suppose that's really how I'm perceived? Am I getting boxed-in? Maybe I'm not being taken seriously. Could it be I need a total change in vocation? I could be a senior pastor! Or possibly just a change in location would do—to a place that's more stimulating, where I'll be forced to grow, and receive needed input into *my* life.

"What's happened to me? Lord, You know I've always wanted to be fighting for the kingdom on the front lines, in the trenches. So what am I doing here? I feel like I'm the guy whose wartime assignment is leading the USO parties. There's no question, I *do* need a change!"

Many Are the Plans . . .

In this frame of mind, a job offer came my way that looked like the perfect solution to my growing dissatisfaction. It was a Christian college setting (still the student world), which involved primarily administration, teaching two courses per semester, preaching on weekends representing the college, and the opportunity to pursue a doctorate degree for which they would pay! I accepted. I signed the contract they offered and presented my resignation to the church's board of elders.

Three weeks later the unthinkable happened. Following a difficult board of directors' meeting centered around an unexpected financial crisis, the college president, who had just hired me, called to inform me that the board was forcing him to renege on my contract. He was upset. I was stunned!

To make matters worse, Valerie was still recovering from the difficult birth of our second son, Justin, and we had just learned that her father was dying. What a time to join the ranks of the unemployed!

I, who was considered "Mr. Make-It-Happen" in ministry, had suddenly become "Mr. Egg-On-His-Face."

Well, the Lord had Steve Bell's total attention! This is an understatement. "God, what are You saying to me? What are You doing?"

I had no alternative but to cry out those verses from Proverbs I had memorized: "Many are the plans in a man's heart, but it is the Lord's purpose that prevails" (19:21). "In his heart a man plans his course, but the Lord determines his steps" (16:9).

"Oh, Lord!"

"MANY ARE THE PLANS IN A MAN'S HEART, BUT IT IS THE LORD'S PURPOSE THAT PREVAILS."

"IN HIS HEART A MAN PLANS HIS COURSE, BUT THE LORD DETERMINES HIS STEPS."

"Steps, nothing, Lord; it's the stops that have me baffled!"

What a Predicament!

"Of all people, how could *you*, Steve Bell, a minister, misread the leading of the Lord?" It was a question I had to face time and again from people in the church shortly after word was out that the position I had accepted at the college had fallen through. My resignation from the church had already been made public, though it wasn't to be effective for another three weeks. What an embarrassing predicament!

In the days that followed, on several occasions my family and I had to make ourselves conveniently unavailable. One weekend we even arranged to go out of town at the last minute just to avoid showing up at what (we fortunately found out in advance) was intended to be a surprise farewell party for us.

"OK, Lord . . . now what? Did I misread what I thought You were telling me to do? I don't think so, but . . . did I?" I continued to process these questions for weeks to come.

During this period of uncertainty and intense soul-searching—egg-on-my-face and all—a couple of issues were still crystal clear to me. I could not deny that there was a restlessness in my soul. I was antsy. I was looking for something more. Staying for almost six years at the same church was unusual for a youth worker. So I was convinced I needed a change, a new challenge—something that would stimulate me to grow and deepen spiritually.

Also, within me—in spite of the awkwardness of my present predicament—was the unquestionable conviction that God was directly involved in all that was happening.

Now nearly fifteen years distant from the situation, it's obvious to me that no mistakes were made. If I hadn't been willing to walk through that "open door" (which very quickly slammed shut in my face!), I may have never learned an incredibly potent lesson.

Looking in the Wrong Direction

During the next weeks I busied myself looking for a "bigger challenge"—jetting here and there, making lots of long-distance phone calls, and checking into other ministry possibilities that had come along. And all during this search the church was gracious enough to put my resignation temporarily on hold. Their patience to allow time for me to process my dilemma was an expression of Christian class and consideration at its finest.

It turned out to be a four-month ordeal. And it finally came to its climax after I had traveled thousands of miles investigating other options, and engaged in seemingly endless phone conversations. The result: I stayed put! I didn't leave the church after all. They rehired me. And my responsibilities remained the same as before.

"You mean that after all the fuss, embarrassment, and personal turmoil, nothing even changed?" It's a logical question to ask at this point.

But actually, things *had* changed!

My inner discomfort was right on target about my *need* for a change. But I had been looking for the solution by directing my energies outwardly. "If my ministry responsibilities were just more demanding . . . If my relationships were more mentally stimulating . . . If others would regularly challenge me or hold me more accountable, then I'd be *forced* to grow. That's what I need!"

Conclusion? Go someplace else. Change jobs.

My thinking was logical. But what I needed, what I *really* needed wasn't a change of location or a change of vocation. What the Lord did for me in those four months was teach me that I needed a change of heart!

It was my focus that was misdirected. My need to deepen spiritually—the lack of growth, the spiritual dullness in my life—was not the result or product of my circumstances or any outside influences. It was strictly a matter of my internal self.

A plaque hung in our kitchen displaying the words, "Bloom where you are planted." Ironically, I walked past that plaque day after day. But its presence had become so familiar, so ordinary, that the punch of its message—*grow where you are*—had escaped me.

I had become so involved with my mission to make Christianity real to teenagers; I had become so caught up in the details of ministry; enthusiasm for the cause had so consumed me that on a personal level my private spiritual life had essentially wilted and dried up.

Fuzz Balls and Paper Clips

Exactly how this spiritual dullness came about—the when, the specifics of the why—I can't fully explain. It occurred almost without my noticing. It's not unlike the fuzz balls that collect under the bed on a hardwood floor, or the coins and paper clips that slip down the cracks in the backseat of a car. When does all of that actually take place? Who knows? Somehow, someway the clutter just manages to accumulate! And that had happened to me inwardly.

Don't misunderstand. My desire to affect the kingdom for good had always remained strong. But the truth is, I had become more open and interested in changing my surroundings and career than in investigating the possibility that the problem might be my lack of inward spiritual discipline. Stated simply: I had lost the intensity of my "first love" relationship with Christ. I was more concerned with my own agenda than God's.

Spiritual dullness is not a matter of outward circumstances as much as it is an inward condition of the soul. The Lord taught me this powerful lesson in a painful, and yes, humiliating way.

With the words, "Of all people, how could *you*, Steve Bell, a minister, misread the leading of the Lord?" still ringing in my ears; four months after I had announced to everyone (and anyone else who would listen) that I was moving on to "bigger and better things" for the sake of the kingdom; after all of this, I found myself in the exact same place—with my wings clipped!

I was learning experientially the truth of the wise words

of the old rabbi who said: "When I was young, I set out to change the world. As I grew older I limited it to my community. Now that I am older and wiser, I see that I should have begun with myself."

Learning to Look Inward

I'm not the only one who's ever looked in the wrong direction to find the needed change in his or her life. I've heard a hundred different versions of my story from others:

- "If only that promotion would come through on the job, then I'd. . . ."
- "As soon as I get a little more money I'm going to. . . ."
- "If I just had a different boss, why I could. . . ."
- "It's my marriage partner who's holding me back. If (s)he had a different attitude, then I know I'd . . . ."
- "If I could somehow get into a group with resources and connections, can you imagine what would. . . ?"
- "Once I complete my doctorate I'll be able to. . . ."
- "When this pressing project gets out of my hair, I'll finally get back to. . . ."

"If only . . . As soon as I can . . . When things are a little different, then . . . " and on and on we talk, plan, intend, and promise. It's a never-ending "mind-set treadmill" commonly used to excuse ourselves from *blooming where we're planted.*

The writer of Proverbs said, "As water reflects a face, so a man's heart reflects the man" (27:19). The condition of your heart, your inward self, is the most accurate reflection of who you are and what you're really like.

Be honest. Is your heart soft and sensitive to the voice of the Lord? Has He been trying to get your attention through some events in your life? Perhaps instead of hearing what He's wanting to say, you're busy blaming your predicament on your spouse, your boss, your circumstances . . . whatever.

Your restlessness, your dissatisfaction with life as it is, in reality could be an indicator that Christ is knocking at your heart's door saying, "Return to Me. Let's spend time together."

Assuming Responsibility

Maybe like me, you need to wrestle with the truth that *Christians experiencing spiritual dullness must learn not to blame outward circumstances, but to assume personal responsibility for it.* For me, coming to grips with this was life-changing.

Again from the Book of Proverbs, "The lamp of the Lord searches the spirit of a man; it searches out his inmost being" (20:27). The fact is, the Lord knows our hearts. He knows everything about us—whether we're blooming, withered and dried up, or somewhere in between.

When the Lord's lamp spotlights the fuzz balls, the loose coins, or paper clips that represent the change that's needed in you, nothing will happen, NOTHING WILL CHANGE, until you take responsibility for yourself. There is no one else to blame for the condition of your heart. NO ONE!

If at this point you're responding, "You're right, Steve. What you're saying is absolutely true," then likely you need to bring yourself to pray the following prayer:

"Jesus, I, and I alone, am to blame for where I am spiritually. I assume full responsibility for myself."

Such a prayer could springboard you from a withered state of spiritual dullness back to your spiritual future—to life and blooming once again!

For Personal Reflection

■ Are there any areas in your life where you occasionally struggle with pride—the unhealthy kind? If so, what are they? (Read Rom. 12:3.) This next step may be hard for you; even so, "swallow your pride" and note those problem areas below:

_____   _____

_____   _____

■ A statement about me that I really dislike hearing from

others is: _____

_____

Think through what it is about the above statement that bothers you so much.

■ Where would you presently place yourself on the continuum below? Mark an "X" representing where you think you fit.

Spiritually content with life as it is. Could not be better!	Experiencing an ill-defined restlessness	Very dissatisfied with life and where I am spiritually
|	|	|

Now evaluate why you placed yourself where you did. What, if anything, needs to change?

■ Reflect on a time when a change in your circumstances did not produce the results you had hoped for. Looking back, what was it that really needed to change?

■ Assuming that God wants *you* to "bloom where you are planted," think of areas where you'd like to experience personal growth. List below as many as come to mind in the next sixty seconds or so:

——————————— ——————————— ———————————

——————————— ——————————— ———————————

——————————— ——————————— ———————————

Invite God's participation to help you select one area where you can begin to focus your attention. He'll willingly assist you. Remember: "The lamp of the Lord searches the spirit of a man; it searches out his inmost being" (Prov. 20:27).

Area selected: ————————————————————

If it's appropriate to your situation, offer to the Lord the prayer at the end of chapter 5. Of course, feel free to revise it as needed to make it more your own.

"Jesus, I, and I alone, am to blame for where I am spiritually. I assume full responsibility for myself."

For Group Discussion

1. True or False: Ministers of the Gospel should be more skilled at perceiving "God's will" for themselves, the church, and others, than should lay people. Explain your answer.

2. Tell about a time in your life (it could even be happening right now!) when you've experienced significant spiritual growth. Describe your life circumstances at the time. Who else was aware of what was happening to you?

3. Everybody needs affirmation along the way. What is the difference between needing some affirmation and seeking recognition? (For some insight into this, read 1 Sam. 18:6-9 and note particularly King Saul's reaction to the situation in the text. From just this incident, how would you assess Saul spiritually?)

4. Think back on a particular incident about which you'd say, "God really had my undivided attention!" Now that some time has passed, has any unexpected good come out of it? Is there a special lesson learned that's unique to that situation?

5. Have you ever literally experienced the "unthinkable"— when a personal dream crashed and burned? If so, describe your feelings at the time. How well did you handle the situation? What kinds of encouraging and/or discouraging comments did people say to you during this time? (Perhaps one or two group members would feel comfortable sharing more specifics. Be careful not to force anyone who's hesitant to talk on this level.)

6. Why do you think most Christian people share more freely about the outward changes they're considering (career move, needed weight loss, car purchase, house improvements, etc.) than they do about the inward (spiritual) changes they'd like to experience? Would you say your conversations at church follow this same general pattern? If so, do you see this tendency as a problem? Why or why not?

7. How closely do you identify with the old rabbi's words included in chapter 5?

   When I was young, I set out to change the world. As I grew older I limited it to my community. Now that I am older and wiser, I see that I should have begun with myself.

   What do you think he's really saying here? Would you agree that this is a Christian concept? Explain your answer.

8. Conclude this session with an extended prayer time. Perhaps group members who are open to this could mention one area in their walk with the Lord where they'd like to experience personal growth, positive change. Focus your prayer time asking God to bring about the desired changes each one has shared. You might do this as a whole group or break into twos or threes, whichever is most appropriate.

Chapter Six

Tearing Away the Mask

KEY BIBLICAL TRUTH:
*Honest self-examination —
reflecting on Jesus' perspective —
leads to personal reformation.*

It was the fall of 1979. The Lord had made it clear to me that what mattered to Him most was my *inner* person—the interior issues, as opposed to the outward circumstances or my place in Christian service.

It's true for all of us. The type of ministry we have, the areas in which we serve, even our scope of influence have little significance in the eyes of the Lord if the condition of our soul is out of whack.

During those months of uncertainty about the future, the Lord reimpressed upon me something that I had already known academically, but had been avoiding experientially. First and foremost, my highest priority and concern must always be my relationship with Jesus!

As the Prophet Samuel said boldly to King Saul, "To obey is better than sacrifice" (1 Sam. 15:22). Or: Obedience to the Lord in the basics is far more important than any kind of Christian service or ministry we can offer.

Spend Time with Me

I had some soul-searching to do. Graciously, the Lord had repositioned me in a situation where I could no longer avoid it. If we had moved, most likely I would have become preoccupied with all the changes in my life—new setting, new people, new job—almost everything would have been different. The adjustments and logistics to make it through each new day would have been all-consuming for at least a year or more. If you've ever experienced a major move, then you know exactly what I'm saying.

However, the Lord intervened (*dramatically* from my perspective), and He kept me in familiar surroundings. In addition, He laid on my heart the charge: "Spend time with Me . . . and grow where you are."

Thus without any distractions and with renewed determination, I began the pursuit. I started searching for more than mere knowledge *about* God. I wanted to go beyond simply understanding biblical principles so that I could explain them in a Bible study or a sermon. Instead, I wanted to interface with the Lord Himself—to experience a private audience with Him.

Like the psalmist I prayed, "O God, You are my God, earnestly I seek You; my soul thirsts for You, my body longs for You, in a dry and weary land where there is no water" (63:1).

A Revealing Light

The late Festo Kivengere, a well-known revival leader and Anglican bishop from Uganda, wrote:

> Jesus Christ is unique, and one cannot be in His presence and not reveal the man he really is. Jesus pulls each person from behind his mask. In the exposure of that bleeding love on the cross, men [and women] become what they really are.
>
> You may think you are wonderful until you stand in the presence of the One who is purity itself. It is the pure light of God that pierces a man. You can keep

up your pretense of being holy until you stand in that light. Then immediately there is nowhere to hide, all your masks are torn away, all your hollow smiles fade.

Revival means to be exposed for what we are. The presence of the Lord is revealing.

What Kivengere was talking about here is exactly what was happening with me—some of my masks were being pulled away. I was keenly aware that my spiritual senses were being sharpened.

I began to see myself differently. Spiritual authenticity became my goal. Areas of my life I hadn't even noticed before began to loom large and were increasingly distasteful to me.

Like Kivengere said, the closer I came to the Lord the more clearly I saw myself and the man I was. "Revival [experiencing spiritual renewal or personal reformation] means to be exposed for what we are. The presence of the Lord *is* revealing."

Seeing More Clearly

And what specifically did I see? I saw:

• Steve Bell, a minister, who was more concerned about program than people. Oh, I cared about people; but the primary way I related to people was to plug them into my program, get them involved, make them feel needed, and keep them busy doing the work of the Lord. I prided myself in the fact that people found it hard to say no to me.

But the Lord got through to me: "Do not think of yourself more highly than you ought. . . . Do not be proud" (Rom. 12:3, 16). "Each of you should look not only to your own interests, but also to the interests of others" (Phil. 2:4). Or said another way: "People *before* program. People *first,* Steve. Start asking what *you* can do for *them.*"

Besides this, I saw:

• Steve Bell, a father, whose two small children had learned to always go to Mommy's side of the bed in the middle of the night when they had bad dreams or weren't feeling well. They learned quickly that Daddy didn't wake up happy. There was no comfort on his side of the bed. Daddy would wake up frustrated, bothered, and mad at them for disturbing his sleep.

But the Lord got through to me: "And if anyone gives a cup of cold water to one of these little ones" (Matt. 10:42) [even if it's your own child and it's the third time the same night!], "Whoever welcomes one of these little children in My name welcomes Me" (Mark 9:37).

And if that wasn't enough, I also saw:

• Steve Bell, a husband, who could unflinchingly take off with his buddies for their weekly Monday afternoon tennis match, leaving behind an upset wife — running a high temperature, sobbing into her pillow — because she's trying to cope with a toddler, a sick baby, and an insensitive husband. "But Valerie . . . I can't let the guys down!"

But the Lord got through to me: "[Husband] . . . be considerate as you live with your [wife], and treat [her] with respect . . . so that nothing will hinder your prayers" (1 Peter 3:7).

Then I also saw:

• Steve Bell, a friend, who was gracious in opening his home to others, but thoughtless and rigid regarding how his schedule and agenda impacted them. To this day I haven't lived down the night when my juices were pumping, and I hammered away on a project in the garage into the wee hours of the morning, while visiting guests (dear friends) were trying to sleep in the room on the other side of the wall!

But the Lord got through to me: "Do nothing out of selfish ambition or vain conceit, but in humility consider others better than [yourself]" (Phil. 2:3). Said differently:

"People first, Steve. The needs of others are more important than your personal agenda."

Even Hearing More Clearly

Not only did I begin to *see* myself differently, but also on one occasion I actually *heard* myself—like I really was!

One evening when I came home from the office, Valerie was sitting at the piano working on some new music. She was completely focused on her singing, but when I entered the room, she stopped and asked me a couple of interested questions about my day. I don't know why, but my responses were sharp and terse.

The incident had no meaning to me until a couple of minutes later. I hadn't realized it, but Valerie was rehearsing with a cassette tape recorder. On the playback as she was innocently trying to find her place to start recording once again, I heard our brief interchange on the tape. I was shocked!

In fact, I was absolutely mortified at my tone of voice. It was awful. I had no idea I was coming off so negative and blatantly critical. Believe me, I would *never* talk to anybody at church like that!

I apologized profusely . . . which only puzzled Valerie. From her perspective, my responses weren't all that unusual. It was simply another encounter with "vintage" Steve.

Unmasking the Real Me

As can be expected from Proverbs 20:27, the Lord's lamp—which searches out our inmost being—was exposing some dark areas in my life. He was unmasking the real me. And what I saw was a man in need of personal revival.

Jesus had a list of legitimate grievances. And not only was I finally paying attention, but also I actually agreed with Him.

Without divine exposure, as humbling as it can be, nothing in our lives will change. We live in delusion until we see our true self—the self that Jesus sees. And such exposure can only be found through an intentional pursuit (as Festo Kivengere put it so well) "of the One who is purity itself."

You may be responding, "Thanks for the warning, but I don't need any more pain or humiliation in my life."

Don't jump to conclusions too hastily because, as strange as it may seem, *I recommend it highly.* In fact, I respect Steve Bell without his many masks a whole lot more than when he wore them.

The best prayer I know for you or any believer in this regard is "Lord, unmask us all!"

God's Gentle Touch

Let me make an important clarification. Without a doubt, had I been confronted with the truth about myself from another person, it could have been devastating. And in all probability my defenses would have flared up questioning the validity of whatever was said. "What does he know? He's got his own set of problems." Or "Who does she think she is?"

But on my own (though the Lord essentially pushed me into it), when I finally admitted to myself that I was spiritually needy and took responsibility for it, when I began to take the time to see myself through God's eyes . . . well, divine exposure was revealing. In a sense it was like experiencing a spiritual x-ray, where the test results were indisputable.

Here's what I found most amazing about this process. Though the list of grievances Jesus had posted at my heart's door was undeniably accurate, I was not devastated. Don't get me wrong. I experienced some painful moments, and at times even shed tears. Overall, however, what was happening in my life was exhilarating. When God's gentle hand is obvious in our lives, even the most difficult of times becomes God-touched.

Spiritual Resurgence

I had encountered divine intervention. I had tried to leave the church to go on to "bigger and better things," thinking that was the answer to my inner dissatisfaction. But God knew better and kept me where I was. And throughout this time in my life, His presence became very real. My personal spiritual life began to resurge.

David's prayer in Psalm 86 captures precisely what was happening within me. Divine exposure brought me to say, "Teach me Your way, O Lord, and I will walk in Your truth; give me an undivided heart, that I may fear Your name" (v. 11).

That's what I wanted—an *undivided heart.* David added, "For great is Your love toward me; You have delivered my soul" (v. 13).

Deliverance! That's what I was experiencing.

Renewed Focus

No longer did my identity depend on the approval of others. The labels people had previously attached to me became meaningless: "Minister of fun . . . The Christian pied-piper with kids . . . The make-it-happen person." These labels lost their power in my life. No longer did they inflate or deflate me.

I was beginning the process toward a more healthy self-image. As youth evangelist Josh McDowell explains it, I was starting to see myself as God sees me—no more and no less.

My renewed focus, above all else, was to please Jesus and to follow hard after Him regardless of the consequences.

I find it ironic now, but as I look back it's apparent that

there was an extended period of time when I didn't even realize I was spiritually needy. I thought I was doing OK . . . even great! However, I had gradually wandered off-center.

No, I never rejected the Lord or denied my faith. I was not immoral, nor in any way unfaithful to my marriage vows. My doctrine never wobbled. I even lived up to my particular subculture's list of religious do's and don'ts. From all outward appearances I was a "kosher Christian."

But with the passing of time, I had lost my spiritual intensity. My first-love relationship with Jesus had gone awry. And this began to show itself underneath the veneer of my life, through a gnawing sense that something just wasn't right.

The Heart's Real Condition

The Prophet Jeremiah challenged God's people, saying, "Let us examine our ways and test them, and let us return to the Lord" (Lam. 3:40).

What Jeremiah suggested in this passage is similar to what most of us do everyday when we look into a mirror. We carefully look at ourselves, and then promptly make all the necessary adjustments before continuing on our way. We primp, we fuss over, we tweak, or (as a last resort) completely redo the hair, the necktie, the eyelashes, the makeup.

Of course, it's much easier to see our outward appearance in a mirror than it is to see the real condition of our heart. To fully see our inner self, we need a supernatural mirror, one that only God can provide.

An Accurate Reflection

Remember the queen in the fairy tale, *Snow White?* She had a mirror with extraordinary powers. Not only could she see herself in it, but also this particular mirror gave her inside information regarding her standing in the kingdom.

"Mirror, mirror, on the wall, who's the fairest of them all?" she routinely asked. Well, one day the mirror responded, "Snow White!" And the queen was devastated. But at least she had the truth. She knew exactly where she stood at that moment.

I believe this is what we need as Christians: An accurate picture of ourselves and our true standing in the kingdom before the Lord. We need to look into such a mirror, God's mirror, and hear what Jesus might say about us. Perhaps we should ask it this way: "Mirror, mirror, *beyond* the wall, is my life pleasing to You at all?"

Imagine how Jesus might respond:

● "Mirror, mirror, *beyond* the wall, is my life pleasing to You at all?"

"Why don't you ever tell anybody about the friendship we have? I care about your neighbors. I care about your associates on the job. My heart breaks because of them! But you never tell them about Me. Since you understand the realities of hell, how can you be so passive? What are you waiting for?"

● "Mirror, mirror, *beyond* the wall, is my life pleasing to You at all?"

"Why don't you have time for Me anymore? You're able to fit in watching television and listening to the radio. You always make time to read the daily newspaper, flip through your favorite magazines, talk on the phone, go out for dinner with friends, serve on committees, exercise at the sports club, play computer games, pursue your hobbies, and take vacations. But, in the course of a day, your thoughts rarely turn toward Me. You've overscheduled yourself with so many activities—life's pace is such a frenzy—that you've crowded Me out."

● "Mirror, mirror, *beyond* the wall, is my life pleasing to You at all?"

"Will you *ever* have enough things to make you happy? Why do you work so hard just to accumulate more and more? It'll wear out. You'll get tired of it. Actually, you look pitiful on that materialistic treadmill. Let Me help you get off. Believe Me, you'll never find peace or contentment running hard and fast just to get more stuff. Stuff does not satisfy!"

• "Mirror, mirror, *beyond* the wall, is my life pleasing to You at all?"

"When did what *other* people think become more important to you than what *I* think? Your preoccupation with the exteriors, your inordinate efforts to appear sophisticated (just to impress people), your intense pursuit of status symbols to achieve upward mobility—none of these things have eternal significance. Please understand: I simply want your heart to remain tender and sensitive to *Me.*"

• "Mirror, mirror, *beyond* the wall, is my life pleasing to You at all?"

"When was it you decided to take control of your life instead of allowing Me to be in charge? You get so wrapped up with your plans, your goals, your rights, and your dreams. . . . Why can't you just *trust Me?* What I intend for you—My dreams for you—are far better than anything you could possibly imagine!"

Can You Identify?

"Mirror, mirror, *beyond* the wall . . . " could go on almost endlessly, and how Jesus might respond affords nearly limitless options as well. So why have I suggested these possible responses? Because when I saw myself in God's mirror, Jesus brought these specific matters to my attention. When I stood in front of the Lord's "Mirror beyond the wall," it's what I heard Him say to me.

If you can identify at all, then you need to set aside some time and find a place of solitude with no distractions. Don't use a busy life as an excuse. Even while driving a car full of grade-schoolers or sitting in a crowded restaurant, you can build a quiet place in your own mind. Go before the "mirror" of God and listen to what Jesus might say to you through the promptings of His Holy Spirit.

If you do what I'm suggesting, I can assure you God will get through. Slow down long enough to let Him speak to your heart. And notice carefully His nudgings.

King David, a man himself who stood before God's mirror, reassured us that God will not despise or ignore "a broken and contrite heart" (Ps. 51:17).

Honest self-examination—reflecting on Jesus' perspective—leads to personal reformation. Said another way, getting back to your spiritual future is the result of transparent honesty before the Lord.

> O Lord, teach us Your ways.
> Give us undivided hearts.
> Deliver us from ourselves!

For Personal Reflection

■ When you're dealing with internal anxiety, an anxious spirit, or a sense of personal dissatisfaction, how do you typically respond? To what or to whom do you turn? Do you prefer escapism to confronting the situation head-on? How open are you to the Lord during these times? (Read Phil. 4:6-9.)

■ You've probably heard a statement similar to this: Who you *really* are is who you are and what you are like when you're sure nobody you know is looking! Assuming this is true, evaluate how you measure up. (Be sure to think through the activities you gravitate toward when you're alone, where your mind goes, the ways you relax and off-load stress, etc.)

Are you comfortable with your responses? How would you feel if your friends at church knew your answers? How do you think God would say you're doing?

■ Circle your answer below: Since becoming a Christian, I find myself offering prayers of confession to God . . .

Regularly   Often   Occasionally   Rarely   Never

■ "Jesus pulls each person from behind his mask . . . " wrote Festo Kivengere as quoted in chapter 6. "You may think you are wonderful until you stand in the presence of the One who is purity itself. It is the pure light of God that pierces a man. You can keep up your pretense of being holy until you stand in that light. Then immediately there is nowhere to hide, all your masks are torn away, all your hollow smiles fade. Revival means to be exposed for what we are. The presence of the Lord is revealing."

Reflect on the last time you experienced the "light of God" (or the conviction of the Holy Spirit) piercing you. What were the circumstances? What was your response? Think back on how you handled it emotionally. Was the result life-changing?

■ What are some issues in your life right now that might be evident were you to pull away some personal masks? Ask God to bring to mind one issue that He wants you to begin to confront.

(For a practical resource that could assist you with this, obtain a copy of the helpful 94-page book *Reversing Self-Destructive Patterns,* a product of The Chapel of the Air, published by Multnomah Press, 1990. Check with your local Christian bookstore, or write The Chapel Ministries, P.O. Box 30, Wheaton, IL 60189.)

■ Before this day comes to a close, set aside some time to get alone with the Lord. Go before His presence, His supernatural "mirror," and listen to what Jesus might say to you through the promptings of His Holy Spirit. Begin this time by prayerfully reading David's psalm of confession (Ps. 51) written after he had committed adultery with Bathsheba. Remember: God will not despise a broken and contrite heart. (See v. 17.)

For Group Discussion

1. Define what a "kosher Christian" looks like in your church setting. Talk about the stated or unstated "list" of religious do's and don'ts common among the believers with whom you fellowship. Are any of these "particulars" extra-biblical and/or unique to your specific subculture? How do you suppose Jesus would respond to the acceptable "list" within your circles?

2. Most people would admit that it's more difficult to be a Christian at home than it is at church. Why is this pattern so common? Do you agree that in reality, this is the result of incorrect thinking? Discuss what needs to happen in our lives to shift such thinking patterns and behaviors.

3. Share with the group a time when some words you spoke "came back" to confront or haunt you! Describe the situation. What did you learn from the incident?

4. Does the church today tend to encourage people to remove their masks or to keep them on? Explain your answer. What, if anything, could happen differently that might contribute to a more healthy environment within your fellowship?

5. A.W. Tozer, a respected American pastor, wrote in his book *The Pursuit of God:*

   I want deliberately to encourage this mighty longing after God. The lack of it has brought us to our present low estate. The stiff and wooden quality about our religious lives is a result of our lack of holy desire. Complacency is a deadly foe of all spiritual growth.

Acute desire must be present or there will be no manifestation of Christ to His people. He waits to be wanted. Too bad that with many of us He waits so long, so very long, in vain.

Every age has its own characteristics. Right now we are in an age of religious complexity. The simplicity which is in Christ is rarely found among us. In its stead are programs, methods, organizations, and a world of nervous activities which occupy time and attention but can never satisfy the longing of the heart. The shallowness of our inner experience, the hollowness of our worship, and that servile imitation of the world which marks our promotional methods all testify that we, in this day, know God only imperfectly, and the peace of God scarcely at all.

Tozer made these observations more than a generation ago. (His book was first published in 1948.) How accurately do you think his words represent the status of the North American church today? Explain your answer.

6. Scripture instructs us that "to obey is better than sacrifice." (Read 1 Sam. 15:22.) However, some believers today substitute a lot of religious activity—busyness—for spiritual empowerment. Why do you think this is a common tendency? What needs to change?

7. C.S. Lewis wrote in *Mere Christianity* (bk. II, chap. 3, para. 7): "God designed the human machine to run on Himself. He Himself is the fuel our spirits were designed to burn, or the food our spirits were designed to feed on. There is no other. That is why it is just no good asking God to make us happy in our own way without bothering about religion. God cannot give us a happiness and peace apart from Himself, because it is not there. There is no such thing."

Discuss the practical implications of what Lewis is saying here for believers today. In light of this truth, what adjustments must we make in the way we live? If time allows, talk about characters from Scripture whose life example would verify the reality of these words.

8. "Mirror, mirror, *beyond* the wall, is my life pleasing to You at all?" is a question that appears repeatedly in chapter 6. Of the possible responses of Jesus mentioned, which one do you most closely identify with? Why? Write out another possible response Jesus might say to you were you to ask, "Mirror, mirror, *beyond* the wall, is my life pleasing to You at all?" (After everyone has completed this exercise, have only those who are willing share what they've written.)

Chapter Seven

Choosing to Take Risks

KEY BIBLICAL TRUTH:
*Getting back
to your spiritual future—
experiencing personal
reformation—requires choosing
to take spiritual risks.*

A significant shift was taking place in my life. I was changing . . . and I knew it! I was paying close attention to what was happening to me. At times it was almost like watching another person.

The Steve Bell I had lived with for so long was undergoing metamorphosis—spiritual reformation. The catalyst to all of this was seeing myself through Christ's eyes, and now I had a fresh awareness of the reality of His presence in my life. I was discovering new motivation to practice old disciplines that had become disinteresting to me.

Previously, I had to force myself to follow through on basic spiritual disciplines. But *now* there was a growing internal spiritual eagerness. Now I *wanted* to be in Scripture. Each day I looked forward to what the Lord might say to me through His Word.

In addition, I experienced renewed interest in prayer. Not only was I privately praying but also I committed myself to meet every week with several other men for an early morning prayer time. No longer was prayer merely the "proper thing to do" before meals and bedtime; it became more than speaking well-intentioned words with spiritual overtones or expressing to God my personal wish list.

Time in prayer meant communing with the Lord—and not just with me doing all the talking. I also spent time listening to the promptings of His Spirit within. This renewed awareness of private audience in the presence of Christ carried with it an incredible sense of privilege, very similar to what's typically experienced when one first becomes a Christian.

Joy in Discipline

Besides a renewed interest in the most basic of spiritual disciplines—Bible study and prayer, my life was becoming more disciplined in other ways. How I spent my time became increasingly important to me. I found television less and less appealing. I began turning it off and started reading more, such as Christian books, professional journals, and other thought-provoking literature. What a huge difference this made! Not only was the input more engaging and stimulating, but also I discovered a growing sense of self-respect. Committing myself to read . . . Read . . . READ . . . was a major step in my new growth pattern.

Carving out time just to be alone then took on fresh significance. Previously, an unstated assumption of mine was. Effectiveness in ministry meant to be always on the go! If there's a flurry of activity, if the schedule is nonstop, if I'm so busy I'm not certain I'll get it all done, something good has to be happening. However, I had mistaken busyness for spiritual empowerment.

Also, because I was now attentive, the Lord drove home the message to me, "Be still, and know that I am God" (Ps. 46:10). It was as if the Lord were saying to me, "You have nothing to say, Steve, until you slow down long enough to actually be with Me—just the two of us."

So I started to build into my schedule "alone time" for prayer, for study, for reflection, for reading, for goal-setting, and for quiet. Yes, even extended times for absolute silence!

Busyness Versus Quality Time

Accomplishing this discipline required some major personal adjustments. You see, I had this uncanny ability to fill every waking moment. God had blessed me with abundant energy, but I can't say I used it efficiently. As long as I can remember I'd never been a morning person. My internal engine would typically shift into overdrive at about 10 P.M., and then I could go strong for another three or four hours. Of course, those hours were hardly my most productive ones.

I decided to try an experiment: Get up earlier. As simple as that might sound, for me that was a *huge* challenge. I made myself do it, though setting up occasional early morning meetings with others did enhance the accountability factor. Literally, I came to discover hours in the day I hadn't known existed before! Initially, this shift in my schedule was quite difficult, but I learned that once I splashed cold water on my face (and found the coffee pot!), I was just fine ... well, almost! It did take a number of months for me to fully realize that I couldn't get involved in some late night, mindless activity (like the midnight reruns on TV or a refinishing project in the garage) and still expect to get up early.

Actually, in the ensuing years I've grown to love mornings — the sunrises, the earth's early dew, and the invigorating freshness of the outdoor air, not to mention the head start on managing the pressures of the day. Previously, I'd always been a night owl, but I was beginning to learn the value of "Early to bed, early to rise." (Ben Franklin was really on to something there!)

Improved Relationships

Besides my use of time, another major change took hold in my life. My relationships were improving. Even my wife began to notice this. Before, my tendency was to dominate conversations and do most of the talking, all the while neglecting to draw out others' concerns or struggles. This "listen to me, I'm-the-life-of-the-party" syndrome fell by the wayside once I channeled that same energy into learning how to ask good questions.

Instead of being so quick to establish who I was, my renewed Christlike mind-set was to show interest in others, to be more sensitive to people. Learning to ask meaningful questions—and then offering a listening ear—helped me shift from a focus on self to an orientation on others.

Shifts in Motivation

It almost goes without saying, the changes I'm describing did not occur overnight, but as an outgrowth of divine exposure—seeing myself as Jesus sees me. With my spiritual eyesight fixed on wanting to please Jesus—with this renewed motivation—I was discovering a new freedom, a new boldness in ministry.

My desire to be a people-pleaser diminished. It was overshadowed by my deepened commitment to realign myself to Christ—to represent His thoughts and His ways regardless of the personal consequences.

I continued in full-time ministry at the church in south Florida until the summer of 1982. So I stayed planted there three additional years after my four-month "resignation" in the spring of 1979.

From my perspective of my nine years at the church, those last three were the most significant because of what was happening to me internally. My personal life was undergoing restructuring and reformation, and the Lord continued to stretch me.

All Things Work Together

In chapter 5, I shared how I had convinced myself that what I needed for spiritual growth was a bigger challenge, more responsibility. But the lesson I really needed to learn was to grow where I was planted. Just as I was getting comfortable with the idea of blooming where I was, another dramatic event took place in my life.

I've always been a sports enthusiast. In fact, my medical records attest to the variety of injuries I've sustained in the pursuit of winning: a series of broken and sprained ankles too laborious to detail; also a serious knee injury with shredded ligaments and torn cartilage. Along with my box of sports trophies, I have another box full of old Ace bandages, ankle supports, knee braces, and three different pairs of crutches. It's a fact of life. Injuries are part of the price you pay in competitive athletics, especially if you hate to lose!

But this next dramatic event was more than I had bargained for.

During the pregame warm-ups in a community winter softball league, and while standing near second base—my assigned position, I was hit on the side of the face, blindsided by a wildly thrown ball. (By the way, the ball used in this sport is anything but soft! It's a misnomer at best—almost an oxymoron.) The ball was probably traveling in the vicinity of 60–70 mph, and when it struck me, it spun me around 270 degrees and knocked me off my feet.

After my face nearly doubled in width size, my teammates immediately rushed me to the hospital. The pain was unlike any I had ever known. Three thoughts were running through my mind: *I am hurt really bad. How are they ever going to fix my face?* And, *Who in the world on our team can throw that hard?*

As it turned out, my right lower jaw was broken in two separate places, the bottom back three molars were uprooted, and the teeth were laying sideways loose in my mouth. After extensive oral surgery, my mouth was wired shut for five weeks. (By the way, it's absolutely amazing what you can eat through a straw!)

I realized it was a freak accident that could have been much more serious. God *had* protected me! But its impact was to be more that just physical in my life.

It was Christmas 1981. Because of the accident, I was given extra time off from the church to spend with my family. Some of that time was spent with extended family— my wife's sister and brother-in-law, Karen and David Mains. I was well aware of David's burden for spiritual revival. In a sense, what I was experiencing personally, David was preaching regularly over The Chapel of the Air's nationally syndicated broadcast. In fact, I wanted for the people in my church what David wanted for the entire country: Spiritual awakening.

As we talked during that holiday season (and yes, it *is* possible to talk with teeth clenched in a wired-shut position), David's dream became my dream. Also mentioned during our conversations was the possibility of someday working together. *Wouldn't that be something, if the Lord was in it?* we thought.

The idea was appealing, though I was aware that buying into this new dream could involve some risk-taking. And what did I know about radio broadcasting? Oh, well, since it would probably never happen, why even worry about it?

Three months later, Rev. John D. Jess, The Chapel's founder and director for more than forty years, informed David of his plans to retire soon. In fact, he set a date just a few months into the future. David realized he would quickly need help on the broadcast and called to offer me the job. David was serious about those earlier conversations! What before had been just a remote idea was now a specific opportunity.

Learning New Lessons

Since we had a tough decision to make, we prayed intensely, "But, Lord, what ever happened to 'Bloom where you are planted?' " It was as though the Lord responded by saying, "Steve, you've learned that lesson. It's time for a new one."

Still I struggled with the Lord: "But I'm not sure I can do it. I don't have a radio voice. It's a field of ministry I've never even considered before. And, God, you know I'm a people person. It's always been my impression that broadcasters are kind of isolated—just a microphone, a producer, and an engineer in a small studio.

"And besides, Lord, we're family! Being related, sometimes that in itself can be a problem. It's a lot harder to gain credibility when you're a brother-in-law to the boss. Plus, it looks like nepotism! I've always made my own way in life.

"Worst of all, what if we can't work together? I really like David. I respect him immensely. But I'd feel horrible if something ever happened to ruin our relationship. I don't know . . . seems awfully risky!"

Dreaming God's Dreams

All of these concerns and questions were legitimate. But after much prayer and a lot of processing, it became clear to me that none of them were the key issues. Again the awareness of Christ's presence focused my attention on the ultimate issue, the predominate question that every Christian should be asking: What is it, Lord, that *You* want?

Another way of asking this is what are *Your* dreams for me? (Instead of What do *I* want? or What do *I* feel most comfortable doing?) The bottom-line question for every believer to ask continually is Lord, what can I do to best advance Your cause and accomplish Your agenda?

With my focus on Christ and His purposes, after several weeks of wrestling with the issue in prayer, searching Scripture, and seeking counsel from my wife and trusted friends, I finally received the answer I needed. I'm sure it's the same answer the Lord's given many of His children down through the ages, at least to those who have hesitated on the brink before jumping into the unknown.

And what was the Lord's answer? It was quite simple: "Trust Me. 'My power is made perfect in weakness.' " These are words that our Lord spoke to Paul (2 Cor. 12:9), and they sealed the decision. I especially like the way the passage reads in *The Living Bible:* "I am with you; that is all you need. My power shows up best in weak people."

Stepping Out in Faith

The Lord used this text to say to me, "Go ahead, Steve. Since you're weak, you qualify. Do it. Step out in faith." It was the nudge I needed.

So in spite of the warnings of well-meaning friends about the dangers of working with family; in spite of my fears of feeling inadequate and of leaving the security of established credibility to start all over again in a brand-new field; in spite of having to uproot my family from south Florida, an area of the country we enjoyed immensely for nine years with its people, its places, and, of course, its weather; in spite of all the logical reasons there were to stay put, the inner promptings of the Spirit communicated to me, "Take the risk!"

I phoned David and said I would join him in his call for national spiritual awakening. For the sake of the kingdom, I stepped out in faith. The Bell family would take the risk.

Taking risks is something most of us do less and less as we get older. Risk-taking always creates the potential for failure. And who's eager to fail? Consequently, for the majority of us, it's a lot more comfortable to maintain the security of status quo than it is to take the chance of being called a fool.

It's easy to fall into this same thinking pattern spiritually. Our tendency is to limit ourselves to the predictable or to that which is comfortable. We're hesitant to venture into new areas of ministry or spiritual growth. We prefer to function in the realm of the usual, where it's safe, where the way is known, and where there are few surprises.

I find it fascinating that most people who are considered significant in the financial world were, at one time, risk takers. They were determined to either make it big or fail profoundly. How much more then should we as believers, with the possibility of yielding dividends of eternal significance, be willing to risk steps of faith.

Understand, I'm not suggesting foolhardy ventures. For example, if you can't carry a tune, don't be too quick to sell out and begin an itinerant music ministry! But when God's Spirit says, "Step out!" we dare not shrink back because of caution or fear. Rather, in obedience, we must be willing to become all that God wants us to be.

A Faith That Risks

In his book, *Revival Praying,* Leonard Ravenhill contrasts the faith that rests with the faith that risks. I suspect (because I've been there myself) that many Christians today are living a "resting faith" instead of a "risking faith." But in reality, spiritual risk-taking should be the *norm* for Christians who are eager to please Christ and accomplish His purposes.

In fact, believers who are undergoing spiritual renewal, those who are on track and growing, are typically spiritual risk-takers. Let me say it even more boldly: *Getting back to your spiritual future—experiencing personal reformation—requires choosing to take spiritual risks.*

According to authors Keith Miller and Bruce Larson, "Renewal [or spiritual reformation] begins when a person is exposed to the forces that will stretch him and help him to discover the power of Christ in the relationships [or areas] where he feels least secure. A church discovers renewal when it preaches and acts in a way which motivates the members to move from their specialties into other dimensions of life."

In other words, an important element of renewal is attempting something that requires God's involvement to accomplish. It might be a new or different personal ministry, or it could even relate to an area of spiritual discipline that up to this point you have purposely avoided. On the other hand, the refusal to take spiritual risks essentially guarantees mediocrity.

Stretching Beyond Your Skills

To ensure spiritual vitality, to help you get back to your spiritual future, let me suggest that you tackle a task that demands God's participation to see you through. Commit yourself to an area of service or discipline that's beyond what you can pull off with your present skills. As Miller and Larson put it, begin moving from your specialty areas into other dimensions. Doing so will force you to stretch!

Don't read me wrong. I'm not suggesting that you have to make a major move or change jobs. Taking spiritual risks can happen exactly where you are.

More specifically, before this day comes to a close, take a moment to go before the Lord and ask Him to point out one area in your life where you can step out in faith and take a spiritual risk. Listen closely to what the Spirit might whisper to you from within.

Which Would He Choose?

Maybe that ministry need you're concerned about within your local fellowship—you know, the problem you can't believe no one has done something about—maybe the Lord wants *you* to be the one to initiate a solution. "But I've never seriously considered that kind of ministry before," you retort. Hey, I can identify with you. But if the Spirit's in it, go ahead! Be courageously audacious. Take the risk.

Perhaps the Lord wants you to share your faith with your employer, your neighbor, or possibly a close relative—or all three!

"But I'm not sure I can do it. That's intimidating!"

I know how you must feel. Of course, there are probably only a dozen or more good books on the topic in your church library. Pick one up. Schedule a talk with your pastor. Develop a strategy. Though your plan may be imperfect, it's a step of obedience worth the risk.

Possibly God's Spirit has been nudging you to teach the Sunday School class that has been without steady leadership for several months now.

"But I don't even like junior highers! I work best with adults."

Could it be the Lord wants to stretch you? It's a wide-open opportunity, and someone is desperately needed. Why not you?

Perhaps the Lord wants your attention regarding how you handle your finances. (Now I know you're getting a little nervous . . . even squirmish.)

"But I don't know how I could possibly exist if I started to tithe."

Or maybe the Lord wants you to break down a wall of prejudice you've been holding on to—racism, sexism, denominationalism, or whatever.

Remember. The issue is what does the *Lord* want you to do? What's best for *His* kingdom?

In Scripture, Peter, a devoted follower of Jesus, encouraged us to submit ourselves to the Lord. "Humble yourselves," Peter wrote. "Under God's mighty hand, that He may lift you up" (1 Peter 5:6). In other words, that He might stretch you and me, that through us He might accomplish His purposes. And when will His purposes be completed? According to this text, "in due time." Or in *His* time!

Think about it. What spiritual risk might the Lord want you to take right now? Consider a variety of possibilities and allow the Lord to seal His choice in your mind.

Come along. For the sake of the kingdom, let's risk together!

For Personal Reflection

■ Think back on a time in your life when you took a risk. What was positive and/or negative about the experience? Would you consider yourself a risk-taker by nature? Why or why not?

■ Read James 4:4-10. Note especially verse 8: "Come near to God and He will come near to you." From this text it's apparent that every believer must take some initiative to build and maintain a healthy, growing personal relationship with God. How good would you say you are in this area of taking spiritual initiative toward the Lord? Circle your response below.

Very good   OK   Not so good   Very poor

■ Understand that the response you noted above has nothing to do with the quality of God's unconditional love for you. In fact, God loves you so much that there's nothing you've ever done or could possibly do that would cause Him to love you any less (or more!) than He does right now. However, the closeness and quality of our spiritual relationship with the Lord is determined by each of us individually. Note what you could do in each of the following basic spiritual discipline areas to enhance your initiative-taking with Jesus:

Scripture reading and study: _____

_____

Prayer life: _____

_____

Sensitivity to the Holy Spirit: _____

_____

Use of time: _____

_____

Personal areas—i.e., habits, leisure, etc.: _____

_____

Relationships with others: _____ _____

_____

Church involvement: _____

_____

Ministry possibilities: _____

_____

Other ideas: _____

_____

■ Take a small risk: Reflect on all the present commitments
that keep your life full and (if applicable) fast-paced, perhaps even stressed-out! Consider which one or two of
your current activities you could possibly eliminate for a
week or so, creating time to focus on a spiritual discipline instead. Write down some options:

Activity that could be temporarily eliminated	Spiritual discipline(s) to be implemented instead
_____	_____
_____	_____
_____	_____

Now determine which option you'll try—and when. It would be ideal if you'd share in advance with a trusted friend what you're planning to do for some added encouragement and a sense of accountability. After your "experiment" be sure to evaluate in a week or so whether or not the "exchange" was valuable. If it was, move on to another option.

■ The following prayer, created through a team effort at The Chapel of the Air Ministries, is helping thousands of believers find the courage necessary to take some spiritual risks. If it represents where you are, begin praying this prayer regularly and make it your own. Invite God to do a work in your life that will cause you to stretch beyond your present personal comfort zones!

Lord,
  Daring to dream again sounds so good,
  But sometimes memories of broken
    dreams haunt me.
  Help me let go of the pain
  That keeps me from responding to
    Your gentle nudgings.
  Your presence encourages me to set aside fear
  And to become a spiritual risk-taker.
  I want Your dreams for me to be my
    dreams as well.
                                        Amen.

■ The following are practical starter suggestions that may help you reestablish some basic spiritual disciplines in your life:

Suggestion #1. A workable plan to get into Scripture regularly is to begin by reading a chapter from the Book of Proverbs that corresponds with the date of the month. For example, on the 3rd, read Proverbs 3, on the 20th read chapter 20, and so on. There are 31 chapters in Proverbs which, of course, coincide nicely with the number of days in most months. Also, since the Book of Proverbs has no significant chronology, it doesn't matter if you read the chapters out of order. Case in point: If you miss a day or two, no problem! Just begin on any given day with the chapter that corresponds with the month's date. By the way, I've found that it's almost impossible to read a chapter of Proverbs without "hearing" the Lord say something to me that's appropriate to my life at the moment. Practical spiritual insights are packed into each chapter! Plus, for me, once I'm reading Scripture, it's a lot easier to keep reading. Begin with Proverbs, then go to other sections of Scripture. Try it for a while. Consider the Book of Proverbs your daily "springboard" into the Word.

Suggestion #2. Another idea that relates to Suggestion #1—and expands it—is to go directly from reading your Proverbs chapter for the day to the Book of Psalms. Proverbs (31 chapters) essentially offers practical insights and godly wisdom for the everyday issues of life, whereas the Psalms (150 psalms/songs) are very worshipful and emotional, heartfelt expressions to the Lord. Combined, these two books provide a healthy, balanced spiritual perspective. Several times a year I find it very beneficial and spiritually motivating to work my way through Proverbs and Psalms monthly. Simply read one chapter of Proverbs and five Psalms daily.

Suggestion #3. It's usually easier to pray with somebody else than it is to pray on your own. This is especially true when you want to establish regular praying as a major discipline in your life. Take the initiative (take a risk!) and find a prayer partner who's willing to commit to meet with you weekly for the primary purpose of praying together. (Perhaps it would be more helpful to meet with several people!) For specific encouragement and a plan of action that's achievable, obtain a copy of the 96-page book *Two Are Better Than One: A Guide to Prayer Partnerships That Work* by David Mains and Steve Bell, published by Multnomah Press, 1991. This practical, step-by-step resource will walk you through the process of finding a suitable prayer partner as well as developing a plan of action. Plus, it includes guidelines and worksheets, along with appropriate Scriptures to focus your prayer concerns. (To acquire copies of this book, visit your local Christian bookstore or write: The Chapel Ministries, P.O. Box 30, Wheaton, IL 60189.)

For Group Discussion

1. Are you a morning person or a night person—or neither? Tell a funny story on yourself related to a time you tried to cross over into the other sphere! Is one "lifestyle bent" better than the other? Why or why not?

2. Share about a time in your life when you took a risk. What was so risky about what you attempted? What impact did the experience have on your life? Why do you think most people tend to take fewer risks as they become older?

3. Differentiate between a legitimate or wise spiritual risk—one that's appropriate or likely to advance the kingdom—and trying something that's literally foolhardy or stupid. (Read 1 Sam. 14:1-14 for a fascinating account of a major risk Prince Jonathan and his armor-bearer attempted. Especially note Jonathan's statement, "Perhaps the Lord will act in our behalf.")

4. Agree or disagree: The refusal to take spiritual risks essentially guarantees mediocrity. Explain your answer.

5. It's frequently said, "Christianity is as much caught as it is taught." Help someone else "catch" a spiritual lesson, by sharing one approach to a personal discipline that works for you. (What you share may be exactly what someone else in the group needs to hear!)

6. C.S. Lewis wrote in *The Weight of Glory*, "Learning in War-Time" (1939), para. 12, p. 30: "The only people who achieve much are those who want knowledge so badly that they seek it while the conditions are still unfavourable. Favourable conditions never come."

When Lewis wrote this he was commenting on the pursuit of education. Apply what he said to getting to know God and developing personal disciplines. Do you think his observation is also true in the spiritual realm? Why or why not?

7. Share how you'd answer the question, "Lord, what can I do to best advance Your cause, and accomplish Your agenda?"

After each person has had a chance to respond, as a group approach this issue another way: Brainstorm collectively how the group could envision answering the above question for each of its members present. In other words, focus on one person at a time, pool your thinking/insights/wisdom about what you know concerning the interests, strengths, and giftedness of each individual, and then answer the same question on behalf of each other.

EXAMPLE: " _____(name of person), we could envision God using you in a significant way to advance His kingdom through _____ " (complete the sentence).

(Who knows what God might put into motion through this process? Keep in mind, though ultimately every individual is personally responsible for his or her own actions before the Lord, often God speaks to us most clearly within the context of community.)

8. Identify one spiritual risk you'd like to attempt in the weeks or months ahead. For those who are brave enough, tell the whole group about your desire!

Chapter Eight

A Strong Finish

KEY BIBLICAL TRUTH:
*Those who run
life's spiritual race well
and finish strong*
deliberately keep in step
with the Spirit.

I n the summer of 1982, my family and I took the plunge! We left the comforts of south Florida. But more than that, we left behind the security of a local church ministry, where for nine years we had felt accepted and loved, to break into a whole new league of ministry—Christian radio.

The Chapel of the Air's daily, quarter-hour program was well-established. Founded in 1939, it was among the early pioneers in Christian broadcasting; and in the truest sense, it is a faith ministry—listener-supported and totally dependent upon the freewill contributions of donors.

Becoming a member of The Chapel's broadcast team was a stretch for me. I had been a fast starter in ministry, but at best a sprinter. Over the past eleven years, however, I have daily confronted the rigors of discipline that accompany broadcasting. Ever present are the nagging pressures of constant deadlines.

Discipline over Ability

I quickly realized that with a shorter message time, word choice is more crucial and preparation time more intense. I have also discovered that natural skills and talent can never substitute for the benefits of long-term disciplines.

It's discipline, not natural ability, that meets deadlines. It's hard work, not spontaneous inspiration, that results in something of value to share with listeners. It's staying-at-it over the long haul that keeps one in step with the Lord, able to represent His thoughts in an accurate and timely fashion.

Many times I've felt inadequate to the task. Repeatedly, I've identified with Moses who bemoaned, "O Lord, I have never been eloquent. . . . I am slow of speech and tongue" (Ex. 4:10). But over the years my courage to stick with it has been rooted in the Lord's response to Moses in this same passage: "Who gave man his mouth? . . . Is it not I, the Lord? Now go; I will help you speak and will teach you what to say" (vv. 11-12).

Since the summer of 1982, I can testify that the Lord has done just that. To date, He has seen me through, though it hasn't been free of pain or without frustration.

Adjusting My Style

I've had to make significant adjustments along the way — less spontaneity and a lot more discipline in my lifestyle, my work habits, and even in the way I communicate. And frankly, I've agonized over some of these adjustments.

For example, everything I say and how I say it is now scrutinized both privately and publicly. Every Chapel broadcast is tape-recorded. As I'm recording, a producer inputs whenever he/she deems necessary. After recording, a professional consultant evaluates each message in writing — what's good and what could be better regarding content, clarity, delivery . . . whatever! Finally, after the program is released "on air" over the nearly 500 daily radio outlets in the United States and Canada, I receive the most important responses of all — letters from listeners. Most of what's written is positive. But also there are those "experts" out there who are helping me become proficient at avoiding mixed pronouns, dangling participles, split infinitives, and other "offensive" grammatical abuses of the English language.

I've never had so much honest feedback in my life! Actually, I've grown to appreciate it, but there have been times when it's been very discouraging.

However, in all of this I continue to sense God's approval. I believe He's pleased with where I am in my personal spiritual journey, though there's still a long way to go.

Let me clarify. For all the difficult or challenging times, there have been many more occasions when I've expressed heartfelt statements like: "Thank You, Lord, for that idea." "That's just the right illustration I'm looking for." "Lord, I'm so glad You led me to this book or to that person." "You really are interested in me and my concerns . . . bless You!"

Since joining The Chapel team, I've become intensely aware of God's personal involvement in my everyday life. The challenge before me now is to cooperate continually with Him to ensure I stay on track spiritually.

Building Endurance

For the past decade, I've been in what I'd call the "catch-up mode." As I have already said, I was a fast starter. I experienced early or "premature" success in ministry that distracted me from developing the necessary disciplines to produce spiritual stamina. But once I found the courage to admit I was needy, when I finally assumed personal responsibility for my spiritual dullness, as I took time to honestly examine myself—to see Steve Bell from Jesus' perspective . . . each of these were critical decisions that were essential to the beginnings of my personal reformation. Without these turning points, I probably would have settled for lifelong mediocrity, and likely never would have gotten back to my spiritual future.

Starters and Finishers

Remember the parable Jesus told about the two sons? (Matt. 21:28-31) Jesus was speaking to religious leaders:

"What do you think? There was a man who had two sons. He went to the first and said, 'Son, go and work today in the vineyard.'

" 'I will not,' he answered, but later he changed his mind.

"Then the father went to the other son and said the same thing. He answered, 'I will, sir,' but he did not go.

[Then Jesus asked those listening] "Which of the two did what his father wanted?"

"The first," they answered.

Jesus said to them [now note how the Master-Teacher put these religious leaders in their place], "I tell you the truth, the tax collectors and the prostitutes are entering the kingdom of God ahead of you."

This is not a passage where Jesus minces words. He had their attention. And what was His point? The Parable of the Two Sons is about starters and finishers. The first son had a lousy start, but finished well. The second son started with a gung ho, "Sure, Dad, I'll be happy to." But then he fizzled out. He never finished!

The first son was like the tax collectors and prostitutes — the spiritual outcasts, who initially reject God, but then gradually come around and end up following hard after Him. The second son is like many in the church today — including some in positions of leadership like I was — initially affirmative, even eager, but then easily sidetracked.

According to one commentator, what Jesus was saying is "All of your verbal affirmations and good intentions, added together, can never equal discipleship."

Pressing On

In a race there are always starters and finishers. Every runner starts, some finish, and fewer finish well. It's discipline that makes the difference. Application? God is looking for starters who are also strong finishers!

Strong finishers are people committed to (what I've been calling throughout this book) personal reformation. That is, these people are eager to maintain a vibrant, active, authentic, spiritual life both present and future. Truthfully, experiencing personal reformation or getting back to your spiritual future is a never-ending journey, a process that's ongoing.

Change, growth, deepening, and spiritual risk-taking are all normative to a vital Christian life. "The best is still ahead" is a valid motto for the believer who holds to this dynamic, spiritually healthy mind-set. Such a person continues to dare to dream, to make God's dreams his or her own. Said differently, there's no retirement plan in the life of faith!

Like Paul, who never stopped growing and never stopped dreaming, we too must get to the point where we can say, "Forgetting what is behind [the successes as well as the failures] and straining toward what is ahead, I press on . . . in Christ Jesus. All of us who are mature should take such a view. . . . [and then in the next verse he challenged us] Only let us live up to what we have already attained" (Phil. 3:13-16).

This is probably where most of us struggle. We may have started the race well. There's no question about the sincerity of our initial faith. But have we gone much further? Are we just a half a lap around the track, winded and out of breath with much of the race still ahead? If so, how can we become strong finishers?

Discipline Makes the Difference

It's become clear to me that fast starters, as I had been, those who can only sprint, will not finish well in a long-distance race. In fact, it's possible for them to get so far behind, to become so discouraged, that they eventually lose interest in the race altogether.

Undoubtedly, most of us have seen, maybe even have known, a spiritual fast starter who had great potential. Such style, such form . . . it was inspiring to watch. Crowds were attracted. Everyone's hopes were high. With his or her natural ability and giftedness, this one could certainly carry the kingdom flag across the finish line!

But then, the letdown. With collective disappointment, it became all too apparent, the runner has become sidetracked. He's dropped out . . . no longer a contender. He's fallen to the cinders, rolling in pain with spiritual shin splints (or "sin" splints), unable to withstand temptation because he wasn't in condition. He wasn't a distance runner after all. He was just another sprinter unprepared for a race that required endurance and stamina.

Or maybe the runner streaked past the stands to the roar of the crowd only to be quickly distracted. In the heat of the race with peripheral vision, she catches a glimpse of the concession stand. She detours to the side, where she joins the other hawkers and vendors in the hope of getting rich. The sound of money jingling at the cash register has a greater appeal to her than plodding along the racetrack eventually to hear the finish-line words of the Lord, "Well done, you strong and faithful runner."

There are a myriad of reasons why believers get sidetracked and fail to run well to a strong spiritual finish. But the root cause in almost every instance is the lack of conditioning, the avoidance and absence of basic spiritual disciplines in everyday life. When such is the case, Christ's presence is ignored and His reality dims for them.

Staying on the Track

At this point in my life, I'm keenly aware of the ongoing potential of becoming spiritually sidetracked. Detours abound. Some are obvious, while others are more subtle and alluring. Most promise an easier path, a less demanding journey. But when taken, they're ultimately unsatisfying. They leave the runner who wants to go the distance spiritually far behind the pack in the dust, having to work hard to catch up. Since I've been there, I'm alert to these dangers.

Today I'm determined to endure, to persevere, and to be a finisher. A strong finisher!

Paul understood the need for endurance. For example, he compared our spiritual life to a race, telling us how we can be sure we're staying on track. He challenged believers to be "running a good race. . . . [and] not gratify the desires of the sinful nature" (Gal. 5:7, 16).

And exactly how is this possible? Paul's answer is "Live by the Spirit" (v. 16). Specifically, Paul instructed us, "Let us keep in step with the Spirit" (v. 25).

We could look at it this way. God has given us His Spirit to be our Pacesetter. He's always with us to help us endure, to help us stay on the growing edge, and to help us run a good race spiritually. Literally, God's Spirit goes before us and determines the pace that will stretch us, but not deplete us. It's up to you and me to follow. And therein lies the struggle since this can be difficult to do. Every ounce of our human nature fights to pull us off course and to launch us off the racetrack in pursuit of our own selfish desires. This is where discipline has to come in.

. Here's what I believe Paul is saying to us, "Those who run life's spiritual race well and finish strong deliberately keep in step with the Spirit." This "keeping in step with the Spirit" has become the primary focus of my life. Oh, how I want to learn to excel in this area!

The Divine Pacesetter

The writer of the Letter to the Hebrews affirmed what Paul taught the Galatians, saying, "Let us [meaning all believers] run with perseverance [that is, discipline] the race marked out for us. [As we run this race] let us fix our eyes on Jesus, the author and perfecter of our faith. . . . so that you will not grow weary and lose heart" (Heb. 12:1-3).

Again Scripture gives us this imagery of the divine spiritual Pacesetter. Jesus has already run this race ahead of us. Although He faced incredible opposition, He finished strong. And as we discipline ourselves to keep our spiritual eyes on Him, we'll learn to recognize the reality of His presence, which gives us needed courage to persist. Specifically, through regular time in prayer, in Scripture, and in worship (both personal and corporate), we become increasingly sensitized to His voice, His nudgings, His choices, and His steps for us.

How would you say you're doing in this spiritual race, this keeping in step with the Spirit? Are you like many who *intend* to keep their eyes on Jesus? You *want* to follow hard after Him, but when it comes down to it, you are easily winded. You just can't seem to press on past the pain of extended conditioning to experience the wonder of significant spiritual growth.

But maybe you're ready to try it again now.

Understand, God is simply waiting for you first to recognize Him as the Great Reformer. You cannot make the necessary changes on your own. It has to be a cooperative effort.

Perseverance in Christ

Before any significant change can take place in your life, like me, you need to admit where you're wrong—where you've detoured or sidetracked. And be specific. Confess that your eyes have not been fixed on the Lord. Detail where your steps have stopped following His. And once you do, get ready to run!

Eric Liddell, known as the flying Scot, was a runner in the

1924 Paris Olympics. He refused to race on Sunday. His unusual convictions became well known since the making of the feature film *Chariots of Fire*. Even the once-in-a-lifetime opportunity to win an Olympic gold medal in the 100 meters, a race he was certain to win, did not sidetrack him from his priority commitment to honor Christ above all else.

Although he didn't run on a Sunday, Liddell did win a gold medal in 1924, setting a new world record in the 400 meters—a race he supposedly didn't have a chance to win. Eyewitnesses who saw him run never forgot it. His style was unique.

"Modern coaches would have been appalled at his running style," writes Sally Magnusson in *The Flying Scotsman*. "It was like his public speaking—poor. His old opponent, Innes Stewart, put it politely: 'Liddell had a curious action, swinging his arms very high, bringing his knees well up, and throwing his head well back.' "

Though hardly a graceful runner, through hard work and perseverance Eric Liddell triumphed over his defects of style.

Like Eric Liddell, I want my perseverance in this race of faith to characterize me. With head thrown back, without concern for what's before me, my goal is to continue to let go—totally abandoned to the race—and finish strong. Though my race may be far from over, someday I want to hear those words spoken at the finish line by my Lord, "Well done, Steve. You've been a strong and faithful runner."

In the meantime, as I look to my spiritual future, I'm determined to stay focused on keeping in step with the divine Pacesetter. I know I have a long way to go and there's still so much to learn.

I hope—and oh, how I pray—that you will join me and thousands and thousands of others in this race *back to your spiritual future*.

For Personal Reflection

■ There are a variety of ways to learn. Identify as best you can your particular learning style. Do you learn more effectively through books, or by listening, by watching, by interacting with others, by doing, etc.? Note what you

think and why: _____

_____

You may find it helpful to share your thoughts with someone who knows you well. Ask whether or not he/she agrees with your self-appraisal.

■ Place an "X" on the following scale that represents your tendency regarding making personal commitments you know will *force* you to stretch spiritually. My typical response to such "opportunities":

Welcome eagerly	Usually open	Occasionally open	Rarely open	Total avoidance

Do you feel good about the answer your mark represents? Why or why not? If not, what step(s) could you take to feel better about yourself?

■ Are there areas in your life where you've been a "fast starter"? If so, list them below:

_____ _____

_____ _____

_____ _____

How would you say you're doing in these areas today?

■ Reflect on an aspect of your life where you've stayed at it over the long haul—i.e., a personal discipline (spiritual and/or physical), a relationship, a task, a ministry, career, or whatever. Detail some benefits experienced because of your "stick-to-itiveness":

_____

_____

_____

■ In light of where you are right now in your personal spiritual journey, in what ways, if any, are you in a "catch-up mode"? Do you feel so far behind the pack that you think you're stuck as is, nothing will ever change?

_____

_____

Remember: Any spiritual discipline, positive habit, or new life pattern has to have a beginning point. Why not now? *You can start your future today!*

■ Begin praying regularly about your spiritual future. Make it a habit! Invite God to stretch you in the area(s) of His choice. Be open to His plans and dreams for you. Ask Him for the wherewithal to keep in step with the "divine Pacesetter." Determine now, in cooperation with the Holy Spirit, to be a strong finisher!

For Group Discussion

1. Discuss your initial response or feelings when you hear the word "discipline." What does it conjure up in your mind? Why?

2. Without mentioning names, describe a spiritual "fast starter" you've known who became sidetracked. (Maybe yourself!) Share specifics about the situation. What do you think caused the person to drop out of the race?

3. Talk about potential detours confronting most believers today that can easily sidetrack us spiritually. On the surface some may be obvious and unappealing, while others are more subtle and alluring. Which are more dangerous? Why?

4. Read Matthew 21:28-32. Which of the two sons in Jesus' parable do you more closely identify with? Why?

   Collectively think of biblical personalities whose lives were similar to the first son in the parable—i.e., had a lousy start but finished well. Now think of characters from Scripture who were like the second son in the parable—i.e., started enthusiastically but then fizzled out and never finished.

   What can we learn from these examples?

5. Talk about the difference between being spiritually stretched and becoming spiritually depleted. Where's the fine line between the two? How can we ensure that we stay on a growing edge without overcommitting ourselves? What might be some possible safeguards?

6. Identify a personal spiritual conviction (like Eric Liddell's refusing to race on a Sunday) from which you could not be dissuaded. Do you think most Christians today take their spiritual convictions as seriously as believers did in earlier generations? Why or why not?

7. In 2 Peter 1:5 believers are instructed, "Make every effort to add to your faith," and then a list of spiritual qualities follows. In verse 8 Peter adds, "If you possess these qualities in increasing measure, they will keep you from being ineffective and unproductive." Finally, in verse 10 we're assured, "For if you do these things, you will never fall."

Distinguish between *our* role in taking personal responsibility for spiritual growth and the role of the Holy Spirit. In what way(s) is it a cooperative effort? (Before answering, be sure to read Gal. 5:13-26.)

8. Share with the group one major lesson learned or personal decision you've made as a result of these sessions together. How can group members best pray for you regarding your spiritual future?